British Gymnastics Olympics

An inspirational read for anyone who loves gymnastics.

Introduction

"Jump off the beam, flip off the bars, follow your dreams, and reach for the stars." These words from five-time Olympics gold medallist Nadia Comaneci ring as true today as they did when she said them.

While many sporting activities require strength, coordination, balance, and determination, very few can combine these traits with elegance, poise, and beauty as competently as gymnastics does.

History is rich in stories of phenomenal gymnasts, but only a thin stratum of them has etched their names into the solid rock of history. Many of the world's greatest gymnasts have been British, and through their hard work, endurance, and unrelenting dedication, they have managed to make their nation proud.

This book highlights stories of their struggles, ingenuity, and hope against all odds to become the best in the world. The book reveals many of the secrets that British gymnasts have utilized to set themselves apart.

Anyone who has a good grasp of the sport knows that British gymnasts do more than compete with the best there is. They also display an unmatched level of technical sophistication.

The book delves into various topics like the history of gymnastics in Britain, the biographies of the best gymnasts in British history, and the various performances at the 2020 Olympics, among other interesting topics.

Let's start with a walk down history lane :

Table of Content

Introduction _____ 2

Chapter 1: History Of Gymnastics _____ 8

The Battle Of The Systems_____10

Who Would Win The Battle Of The Systems? ___11

Women's Entrance Into Gymnastics _____14

Popular Types Of Women's Gymnastics Today _16

List Of Gymnastics Moves_____24

Are There Risks Involved In The Sport? _____30

Chapter 2: History of the Olympic Games _34

The Return Of The Olympic Games_____37

The Modern Era _____39

The Olympic flame _____40

Gymnastics As A Part of The Games _____43

Memorable Olympic Games Moments For Gymnastics_____70

The Olympic Games Versus The World Championships ___75

Where The Olympics Stand Today ___76

Chapter 3: GB Gymnastics in the Olympics Over The Years ___78

The 1928 Team ___79

Great Britain At The 1936 Women's Gymnastics Games ___81

1948 Games in London ___82

The 1952 Games In Helsinki ___84

The 1956 Games in Melbourne ___84

The Great Drought ___85

The 2012 London Olympics ___85

The 2016 Olympic Games ___89

Chapter 4: The Build-Up To The Tokyo 2020 Olympics ___92

The Japanese Bid ___92

The Emergence Of COVID-19 ___97

Short Biographies of Participating British Gymnasts ___102

Getting Close to The Big Date ___112

Chapter 5: The Tokyo 2020 Olympics Experience And Final Scores ___115

COVID-19 Health Measures ___116

Qualifier Rounds ___116

AA/Individual Finals ___132

Women's Floor Finals ___134

Team Final Bronze Medal Moment ___141

The Rest of the British Performances in the Finals ___148

Interviews From The Team ___154

Chapter 6: Motivation For Aspiring Gymnasts ___161

Why Get Into Gymnastics? ___161

How Gymnastics Empowers Women ___165

What Would It Take To Get To The Olympics? 168

Is There an ideal Gymnast Body? _____169

Find The Right Coach You Trust And Can Work well With _____170

How To Avoid Physical Injuries In Gymnastics 173

Gymnastics And Good Mental Health _____176

Tips For Becoming The Best_____181

Conclusion _____189

Chapter 1: History Of Gymnastics

"If you're having fun, that's when the best memories are built."

Simone Biles

What did the great playwright William Shakespeare have to say about gymnastics? *"To BEAM or not to BEAM, that is the question...."* The corny joke aside, this quote highlights Britain's pressing question in the late 19th century.

Today, the whole world marvels at amazing gymnasts, and we assume that gymnastics was always destined to be a great sport. However, the truth is that in the not too distant past, the sport as we understand it today didn't even exist. It took the efforts of several determined individuals to make it into the sport that we all love today.

As the sport we know today, gymnastics was started by Fredrick Ludwig Jahn in the 1800s to help improve the health and fitness of German soldiers. However, it is worth noting that earlier versions of the sport also existed in ancient Sparta. To this day, you can still find the remnants of this ancient and glorious city on the eastern foothills of Mount Taygetos in Greece.

It's easy to understand why gymnastics as an activity could be of value to soldiers. The sport requires body strength, an enduring soul, and a sharp mind. The sport also improves physical coordination, reflexes, and flexibility. These qualities can form the critical difference that saves a soldier's life.

Given that soldiers are only interested in utility, not aesthetics, it took a while before gymnastics became appreciated as a sport with the elegance and beauty we appreciate today.

In the late 19th century, the popularity of gymnastics gradually spread throughout Europe and especially in Sweden, but the sport was still considered rather small. Britain had a choice to either ignore the rapidly developing movement of gymnastics or commit to trying it out.

At the time, the sport had two main variations: the German and Swedish versions of gymnastics. It would be many decades before there was a resolution to the dispute between these different ways of doing things.

The modern British Amateur Gymnastics Association, or BAGA for short, was formed in 1888. However, it was a different name because fencing and gymnastics were under one umbrella. The organization held tournaments where competitors would show off their skills and compete against other talented individuals.

The Battle Of The Systems

Around this time, the rivalry between the German and Swedish versions of gymnastics had developed into a war.

This conflict would come to be known as the Battle of the Systems. The popularity of the two systems varied from one region to another, with people moved by and influenced by fashions, myths, and personal preferences.

Pehr Henrik Ling started the Swedish version —also sometimes referred to as light gymnastics because it utilized no apparatus and focused more on exercises and calisthenics. The Swedish version was considered freer, less regulated, and focused primarily on health benefits.

On the other hand, the German version utilized apparatus — like bars, beams, and rings— and vaulting. It had a very "militaristic" feel and emphasized strength, discipline, formality, and rules.

There were two other competing systems: the Delsarte and the Sargent system.

Frenchman Francois Delsarte created the Delsarte system. As one might expect from the French, the system emphasized elegance, grace, beauty, and poise. This system was particularly popular among dancers, theatrical actors, and physical education teachers.

On the other hand, Dudley Allen Sargent, an American director of physical training, created the Sargent system. He incorporated some of the attributes of the German system and a few of the Swedish and then added unique adjustments to the system. Dudley personally constructed many of the apparatus used in his system. Something unique is that Dudley factored in anthropometric measurements into his system.

Anthropometry is just a fancy word for human measurements such as height, weight, and size. These factors vary from person to person and impact how a gymnast performs. These factors even affect an individual's probability of getting injured. For example, shorter individuals tend to get hurt less when engaged in gymnastics. A medical examination was a requirement before engaging in the Sargent system. Therefore, Dudley was well ahead of his time in that particular regard.

Who Would Win The Battle Of The Systems?

Determining who won the battle of the systems is a far more difficult question to answer than one might expect. Various political and cultural factors came into play that caused an unexpected ebb and flow between the various systems.

Today, the International Gymnastics federation sets standards and rules for gymnastics, also known as Fédération Internationale de Gymnastique (FIG), in French. Despite being established in 1881, the organization had little influence because most countries didn't join.

In the late 1800s and early 1900s, standards and rules in gymnastics varied widely from one region to another based on fashions and cultural differences. For example, the more militaristic versions of gymnastics were not very popular with some people in the upper classes of America and Britain. That is because the strenuous nature of the German version of gymnastics led to protruding muscles and an overly buff look, something considered unrefined and even vulgar at the time. Some wealthy individuals preferred the softer versions of gymnastics that created physical fitness and good health without excessive muscles.

As gymnastics started becoming popular in schools as a part of physical exercises, many educators also advocated for softer versions of gymnastics that didn't strain their students.

After the First World War outbreak, there was a shift in opinion as people began to value a strong muscle look. Nice aesthetics weren't going to help anyone in the battlefields of the war, so people shifted their views to value strength and muscles rather than a pleasing slim look.

After the end of the war and as people settled back into normal life, there was another shift as softer versions of gymnastics became popular again.

We can best describe the battle between the various styles as having ended in a compromise. The German beams and rings are used widely today at international competitions, but nobody can deny that French beauty, elegance, and poise are present in gymnastics today.

Likewise, the Sargent system created by Dudley Allen Sargent was far ahead of its time in highlighting the importance of Anthropometry and medical examinations, both of which are a part of the sport today.

Today there are six distinct types of gymnastics, namely:

1. Artistic gymnastics
2. Rhythmic gymnastics
3. Acrobatic gymnastics
4. Group gymnastics
5. Trampoline

6. Tumbling

We shall discuss more on this later:

Women's Entrance Into Gymnastics

At its inception, modern gymnastics was entirely male-dominated. Its military use in Germany meant that only men practiced it because there weren't any women in the military at the time.

When gymnastics eventually caught on for women in the 19th century, it primarily focused on two critical issues.

The first objective was to foster good health, specifically regarding the female anatomy. Many women hoped to heal gynaecological issues, purify their blood and raise their digestive organs. Some of these beliefs weren't really based on scientific evidence, but this didn't stop folks from believing them.

The second reason women got into gymnastics was the belief that it encouraged women to adopt the anatomical characteristics of Venus de Medici. This is a Hellenistic statue standing at 5 feet, and it depicts the Greek goddess of love named Aphrodite. For centuries this statue has been epitomized as the ideal of perfection as far as female beauty is concerned, and so any activity that could help women achieve this form was worth the effort.

The fact that many women weren't engaged in sporting activities before the late 19th century wasn't entirely because of discrimination or cultural limitations placed on women.

Before the industrial revolution, most people's living standards were simply far too low to allow for activities that could be categorized as leisurely. When you aren't sure about where your next meal will be coming from, you aren't going to be wasting calories on sporting activities.

It wasn't until the industrial revolution took off that an explosion in wealth could allow for the emergence of a middle class that had extra time, money, and calories to burn. This is why gymnastics among women emerged strongly within the middle class before becoming popular with other social classes. Many people simply called it calisthenics instead of gymnastics because the word had strongly effeminate associations. The term calisthenics translates from Greek to mean beauty, which made the word preferred to the rougher-sounding gymnastics.

A surprising factor that influenced the popularity of gymnastics in Britain was religion. In the late 19th century and early 20th century, a growing number of Christian thinkers felt that society was becoming too soft and complacent. The wealth created by the industrial revolution was alleviating poverty, and this was a good thing, but nobody could have predicted that this could lead to physical laziness.

In response, various activists such as Thomas Hughes called for a new type of Christianity that emphasized the "discipline, self-sacrifice and the moral and physical beauty of athleticism."

In response, public schools in England started incorporating physical activities, including gymnastics, as a patriotic duty act. This introduced many young girls to gymnastics based on this emerging trend of the time.

Popular Types Of Women's Gymnastics Today

There are three main female-friendly gymnastics forms: aerobic, rhythmic, and artistic gymnastics.

What is rhythmic gymnastics?

Rhythmic gymnastics utilizes dances, movements, and various apparatuses to create beautiful displays. Only women can compete in rhythmic gymnastics, and they usually use balls, hoops, ribbons, and ropes.

What is aerobic gymnastics?

Aerobic gymnastics–also called sport gymnastics– involves performing routines by individuals, duos, trios, or even groups of six people. Such routines involve using muscles, which is why this gymnastics emphasizes strength and aerobic fitness.

What is artistic gymnastics?

The third form of gymnastics and the primary focus of this book is artistic gymnastics. This is a form of gymnastics where athletes perform short routines using apparatus specifically designed for a particular activity. Both men and women compete in artistic gymnastics.

While rhythmic gymnastics focuses on elegance and aerobic gymnastics focuses on strength, artistic gymnastics is well-rounded. It requires an assortment of qualities like power, agility, balance, control, coordination, and elegance.

Men in artistic gymnastics compete in six categories. The categories are floor exercise, pommel horse, still rings, vault, parallel bars, and horizontal bars.

Men's and Women's Artistic Gymnastic Categories

These are categories that both men and women engage in at international games;

• Floor exercises

In floor exercises, gymnasts perform routines on a specially prepared exercise surface –counted as an apparatus. The springboard helps provide "bounce" for the gymnasts while simultaneously helping avoid injury to their legs and body if they happen to fall. Floor exercises typically tend to last for a total of 90 seconds. Gymnasts can express their passion and personality through their dance and musical choices.

The judges use the D-score –also called the difficulty score system– to award points based on the difficulty of the routine performed. The D-score is calculated by adding values for 8 of the most difficult, connections, skills, and compositional requirements.

D score chart

A	0.1
B	0.2
C	0.3
D	0.4
E	0.5
F	0.6
G	0.7
H	0.8
I	0.9
J	1.0

On the other hand, the E score measures the quality of execution of a particular skill. It might be tempting for a gymnast to go for very complex routines to get high points for difficulty, but this can easily lead to poor points for execution. Point deductions, perhaps due to poor form, falls, or mistakes like stepping outside the designated parameters can worsen this.

A routine can be made up of turns, leaps, dancing, and up to four tumbling lines. At international competitions, a floor routine must have a minimum of:

- Double saltos/somersaults

- Saltos/somersaults with a minimum of one twist

- Connections of two dance elements with one that is at least 180 degrees

- Saltos, either forward, backward, or sideways

• The vault

Friedrich Ludwig Jahn, a German gymnastics educator/nationalist, invented the vault. It works by using two spring boards to help gymnasts increase their jumping distance. This is done by having them run fast, jump on a spring board on the floor, then turn their bodies 180 degrees so that they can then use the hand spring to lodge their bodies even higher and perform manoeuvres in the air earn them judges' points.

Every vault has four critical stages:

1. A running start
2. Leaping off a springboard
3. An athletic manoeuvre that involves a vaulting horse
4. A landing

A vaulter is judged on many factors, including proper height, body alignment, repulsion, form, distance travelled during the flight phase, saltos, and twists.

Men only artistic gymnastics categories

These are categories that only men compete in at international games;

• The pommel horse

This is a device usually used by men. It is made of a metal frame with a leather cover. Two protruding handles emerge that can be used for manoeuvres. It was designed in Roman times as a way to teach horse riding.

A routine on it must include;

- A single horse swing
- A dismount
- Circles and flairs
- Side or cross support travels

Success at this requires individual competitors to keep their feet and legs straight during an entire performance which can be extremely challenging. Points are deducted for stopping or pausing while on the device.

• Still rings

This is a device usually used by men. The two rings hang freely upon two straps attached to a strong metal frame. The gymnasts hold the two rings, lift their bodies, and control their movements while holding the rings in the air.

• Parallel bars

Two long positioned wooden bars are parallel to each other at the height of 11 feet. A gymnast stands between the two bars and uses them to lift their bodies before elevating themselves and performing movements on the bars with their hands clasped on.

• The horizontal bar

This is a single cylindrical metal bar, also known as the high bar, due to its height above the ground. The bar is used by athletes who perform manoeuvres on it, such as rotating, releasing, and re-grasping the bar.

Women only artistic gymnastic categories

For female gymnasts, there are two categories that only they can compete in at international games;

• Uneven bars

Uneven bars are made up of two steel frame bars. One bar is higher than the other. A gymnast performs routines while using their hands to hold the bars and move their body from one bar to the next.

• Balance beams

The balance beam, also called the beam, is a thin beam raised above the floor on two steel legs. The beam is covered with leather material and is only four inches wide. Gymnasts perform leaps, dance poses, and handstands on the beam.

List Of Gymnastics Moves

The chapters that follow will involve descriptions of routines performed by British and other international gymnasts. To ensure you can understand these routines, it will be necessary to grasp a number of basic moves that can be performed in different types of gymnastics categories. Without understanding these moves, it will be difficult to grasp why one gymnast would win more points on the difficulty score over another gymnast. Here they are:

Splits

This involves a gymnast splitting their legs sideways or front-and-back to a point where their whole lower body, including their legs and rear end, is in contact with the ground.

Handstand

This involves standing on one's hands as opposed to one's legs. The whole body is straight, and the toes point upwards.

Handspring on vault

This begins with a gymnast running leap followed by a flip into handstand position on a vault and then pushing off the vault to complete a revolution and land on their feet.

Turn on one foot

This is a pivotal rotation executed on a beam on a dance floor.

The back handspring/ Flick / Back flip

This is a backward flip of the body, where the gymnast lands on hands and the legs then follow in the same direction as a pair. It ends with the gymnast returning to a standing position.

The front handspring /Flick / Front flip

This is similar to the back handspring. However, this time, the gymnast moves forward.

The cartwheel

This is a sideways manoeuvre in which the athlete turns their body using their hands upon touching the ground, quickly followed by landing on their legs in a similar sideways manner.

Aerial cartwheel

This is also called the side flip. It is similar to an ordinary cartwheel. However, the gymnast's hands do not touch the ground this time. The athlete has to generate enough momentum while turning sideways to turn their whole body in the air before landing.

Backwards somersault

This is a backward rolling movement on the floor in which the athlete tucks in the knees to create a round-like body shape capable of rolling.

Forward somersault

This is the same as a backward summersault. However, the gymnast rolls forward after crouching and tucking their legs into their abdomen.

Aerial walkover

An aerial walkover, also known as a front aerial walkover, involves jumping and executing a complete 360 degrees turn of the body while in the air and then landing on the same spot.

Round off

This involves turning the body forward like a cartwheel, but instead of moving sideways, the gymnast turns their body forward. The gymnast should not leap during the round-off, and the second foot should only leave the floor when the first hand touches the ground.

Scissors leap

This is a leap in which the gymnast's legs exchange their positions while still airborne to execute a split in the air.

Split leap

The straight jump is when a gymnast puts one leg in front of another, stands on their toes, bends their knees, and leaps into the air. The legs must stay straight when in the air and when landing.

Cross handstand

The gymnast places hands close to each other over the width of the beam. Her stomach faces the length of the beam, and then the legs go up closed in the handstand position.

Yurchenko

This move is named after gymnast Natalia Yurchenko. It is popularly impressive for combining multiple manoeuvres at the same time.

It begins with a round-off onto the spring board, then a back handspring on the vault. It ends with a backflip off the vault to reach the floor.

Back walkover

This is a complete revolution of the gymnast by moving their upper body backward until their hands reach the ground to create a back bridge. Their legs then turn backward, one after another, until the gymnast is in a standing position again.

Front walkover

This is similar to a back bridge, but the gymnast moves forward to complete a full revolution.

Tsukahara

This move is named after Japanese gymnast Mitsuo Tsukahara. It involves making a round off entry on the vault and then dismounting off the vault using a backflip.

The mount

This is the simple process of getting onto any piece of apparatus. This is doable by simply hopping onto it, jumping over the low bar, or performing a flip before catching the bar.

A bar routine

A bar routine is the description of the moves performed on uneven bars.

15-20 moves should be performed without pausing; they involve both the high bar and the low bar.

The dismount

This is the process of getting off the bars/beam and vault when the routine is completed or the final tumble pass in floor is referred to as the dismount.

Bar change

This is moving from one bar to another. During a routine, a gymnast must move between the low and high bar at least twice. This can be executed by performing a flip from one bar to the next or simply placing their feet on the lower bar and then jumping to the high bar.

Shaposhnikova

This is an uneven bar move. It starts with a hip circle on the low bar past the hand-stand position to a flight release with a full twist, i.e., 360°, before catching the high bar. When performing a full-twisting Shaposhnikova, a gymnast will begin on the low bar with her back to the high bar.

Amanar

The move consists of a round-off onto the springboard, then a back handspring onto a vaulting platform, and into 2½ twists in a back layout salto off the table.

Are There Risks Involved In The Sport?

A common question on the minds of many aspiring gymnasts is what dangers exist in it. They wonder if they should go into a sport that could put their bodies at risk.

Physical risks associated with gymnastics

Watching a gymnast on a beam can be an exhilarating experience. A small part of the excitement has to do with the fact that there is an element of risk associated with artistic and aerobic gymnastics routines.

It is human nature to admire people who are courageous enough to do things most people are too afraid to do. Gymnasts at international competitions have had broken wrists, cartilage damage knee injuries, to name a few. Other physical risks involved in gymnastics include hand injuries, tearing of the Achilles tendon, ankle sprains, and even herniated spinal discs.

A famous example of a physical injury was Adrienne Nyeste's fall at the Sydney summer games of 2000. While performing on uneven bars, she slid off the bars and fell, face-first, into the ground. Sounds of concern were immediately heard from the crowds, and the fact that she lay motionless on the ground for a few seconds caused concern from everyone. Despite an injury to her face, she stood up, dusted herself off, and recovered from the fall.

The truth is that most sports always carry a risk of physical injury, a simple fact that gymnasts have come to accept over the years. The exemplification of courage at gymnastic performances helps the athletes to overcome their fears, and they inspire people watching them to dream a little bigger and aim a little higher.

Over the years, officials at FIG have taken the safety concerns of athletes, coaches, and parents into consideration. Changes have been made to improve the safety of the sport.

An example of this is that, in 2001, changes were made to the vaulting horse. It used to be much thinner than it is today, but this was changed to allow for greater room to work with.

This was necessary because gymnasts flying backward into the horse would sometimes miss it.

Psychological risks associated with gymnastics

Beyond the physical pressures involved in the sport, there are also many psychological pressures.

The teenage years are challenging without the added pressure of needing to keep up with a rigid exercise schedule, especially because many gymnasts need to practice for at least 30 hours a week. Gymnasts have to carve out time in the early morning or later in the afternoon to sharpen their skills and stay on top of their game.

The anxiety that comes with performing gymnastics is significantly greater for gymnasts operating at an international level. Patriotic feelings from millions of people waiting for you to bring home a medal can be too much for some young gymnasts to handle.

For professional gymnasts, the challenges involved with traveling to attend competitions in faraway environments filled with new people can also add some pressure to the job.

A few journalists and experts have called for raising the age at which teens are allowed to participate in events like the Olympics. As it stands, an aspiring Olympian must be 16 years of age to be able to compete in gymnastics. This age has been called into question due to several psychological factors.

One is that young Olympians have had anxiety issues that have led them to feel overwhelmed. An example would be in the Tokyo games when one famous gymnast dropped out from one of the competitions, citing mental health issues. We shall talk more about it in chapter 5. However, it suffices to say that her dropping out led retired gymnast and two-time Olympian Alexandra Raisman to state that the event was a sobering reminder that "*Olympic* athletes are human." She implied that people don't understand the pressure athletes can endure in such competitions.

How to deal with these risks

There are ways of dealing both with the physical and psychological challenges of the sport. Gymnastics should be a source of joy and relaxation, not angst or injuries.

Gymnasts who want to get the positive aspects of the sport and avoid the negative need to be equipped with the right skill set needed to cope with the challenging aspects of the sport. Chapter six will offer a way forward regarding both physical and mental health.

Chapter 2: History of the Olympic Games

"An Olympic medal feels absolute magic."

Alice Kinsella, British gymnast

The Olympic Games were first held in Ancient Greece to honour the Greek gods and, in particular, Zeus, the King of all the gods. Therefore, the games were primarily a religious festival at the sanctuary of Zeus in Olympia.

At the time, Greece was divided into various city-states that were often at each other's throats for one political reason or another, but these differences would often be set aside for the games to be held.

This period of peace could, at times, mean a temporary end to wars because no city wanted to incur the wrath of the gods by failing to honour Zeus at the appropriate time. This period of peace was known as the Olympian peace.

The games held were both athletic and combat. During this period, war was a common occurrence between the various city-states and neighbouring hostile powers like the Persian Empire. As such, the Olympic Games placed great value on martial and physical prowess because their freedom and lives depended on these attributes.

The origin of the games themselves was shrouded in mystery and legend even amongst the Greeks themselves. The most popular legend at the time was that Zeus ordered that the games be held every four years, and his son Heracles named the games Olympian. The myth also states that Heracles completed the 12 labours and then built the Olympian stadium himself. Following its completion, he walked 200 steps and called this unit of measurement "stadion."

Rationalistic-minded archaeologists and historians not interested in fables about gods instead choose to believe that the games must have begun earlier than 771BC based on archaeological evidence found inscribed at Olympia, where inscriptions about athletes were written down. These inscriptions have information regarding winners in a couple of competitions that took place at the time, such as wrestling and foot racing.

The sporting events would often go hand in hand with ritualistic sacrifices of animals to the gods. This was a custom that was prevalent worldwide at the time. The statue of Zeus decorated the temple halls at Olympia and was one of the wonders of the ancient world. Another statue was of King Pelops, a divine, mythical king known for competing in a chariot race against King Oenomaus of Pisa.

It's tempting to think that the kinds of games played millennia ago by the ancient peoples of Greece would be drastically different from we modern folk, but this is not entirely true.

Some of the games held at the time included running, which consisted of the stade race of 200 meters, and two stades, which constituted 400 meters. Another sport was the pentathlon which consisted of five competitions performed by five different athletes. The discus throw that's still part of the Olympics was also very common back then. Boxing, wrestling, and jumping were also part of the event.

The popularity of the Olympic Games continued to grow until their peak in the 5th century BC. After the conquest of the Greeks by the Romans, the games gradually lost significance. The emperor Theodosius II decreed that all foreign worship of gods and cults be banned from the Roman Empire. And so, the games that had been a part of the worship of Zeus lost significance. In fact, most Greek temples were destroyed on the emperor's orders, so the Olympic Games as a phenomenon would die out for several centuries to come.

The Return Of The Olympic Games

In the 17th century, the word "Olympic" came back into use when referring to competitive games. This could have been due to the overall fascination with Greek culture that followed the renaissance period when everything Ancient Greek was a matter of fascination and fashion.

An example of this was the Cotswold Games – also referred to as the Cotswold Olimpick Games. The competition was held once a year in Cotswold, England, from 1692 until 1852, when it ended; fortunately, the games were revived again in 1963.

The games came into being because a local lawyer called Robert Dover, with the approval of King James I, insisted men needed to engage in physical exercise if they were to be fit enough to defend the realm.

In 1796 France, the government attempted to return the games in an event called *L'Olympiade de la République*. The event aimed to imitate the ancient games as well as possible.

In 1834 Stockholm, Gustaf Johan Schartau organized another attempt to return the Olympic Games. The games were considered a phenomenal success as they drew a crowd of over 25,000 people, which was quite an accomplishment given that there were no modern means of transportation by which people could travel to go and watch the games.

In Liverpool in 1862, there was another attempt to restore the Olympic Games. It's interesting to note that the British made more attempts to restore the Olympic Games than any other nation did, including the Greeks. Perhaps this speaks to the strong ethos of competition and sportsmanship found in the British people. The leader of the Liverpool attempt was a man named John Hulley, and it was aimed at gentleman amateurs but hoped to draw people from other parts of the world.

In 1850, a surgeon and magistrate called William Penny Brookes decided to open an Olympian Class at Much Wenlock, Shropshire, England. Later in 1859, Brookes decided to name the class Wenlock Olympian Games. This annual sports festival is still held today.

In November of 1860, Brookes founded the Wenlock Olympian Society. This information is relevant because it will help you understand how the body that governed Olympics worldwide came into being.

After attending the Wenlock Olympian Society's Olympian Games of 1890, Baron Pierre de Coubertin was so enthralled by the various performances that he decided to create the International Olympic Committee (IOC).

The Modern Era

At this stage, one might wonder what the Greeks themselves thought about all the various attempts at restoring the ancient and glorious Olympics. Many of these copycats didn't even bother to invite the Greeks to compete in their games. It would be understandable if the Greeks felt a little left out and angry about things.

However, one problem the Greeks had was that they were still living under the Ottoman Turkish Empire's control and couldn't quite return to their culture just yet. It was not until 1821 that they gained independence and could seriously start thinking about the Olympics, and even then, there was still the problem of money.

In 1833, a wealthy Greek philanthropist wrote to the King and told him that he would be willing to fund the Olympics if the King gave his blessing. The philanthropist named Zappas funded the Olympics in 1859, held in Athens. Zappas funded the construction of the ancient Panathenaic Stadium to start hosting Olympic Games in future. The stadium hosted the Olympics in 1870, where 30,000 people attended. Interestingly the Olympic Games in Greece copied many aspects of what they saw in the Wenlock games rather than simply coming up with their way of doing things.

The Olympic flame

The Olympic flame is the single most famous symbol associated with the Olympic Games. It represents the continuation of the games from the time of ancient Greece to the modern world. However– and disappointingly–contrary to popular myth, the flame does not come from an ancient fire.

Like many aspects of the games, the idea to use a flame was copied from the Greeks, who used to have a fire lit throughout the games in ancient times. The flame was part of a religious ceremony in which the flame was lit in the temple of Hestia.

Today, 11 women representing the vestal virgins of ancient Greece light the fire according to past ceremonies. The fire is not lit using matches or natural gas but rather using the sun's power. This gives the ceremony a sense of being connected to the past.

At the first modern Olympic torch relay, the flame was transported from Olympia in Greece by runners who ran for 12 days and nights to reach Berlin for the summer Olympics of 1936 to cover a distance covered was 3187 km.

The route chosen for the Olympic flame goes through areas that have aspects of great human achievement, which is meant to show tribute and respect for these accomplishments. The flame first travelled by boat in 1948 and by plane in 1952 when it was flown to Helsinki.

Various other unique methods of transporting the flame have been used, such as riding a camel and using a Native American canoe. The torch itself has even been taken to space on three separate occasions, but unfortunately, the flame was off as a safety precaution against starting fires on board the rockets. The London underground train and undersea divers have also the flame's transportation or ignition.

In 2004, the flame was first transported across the globe for 78 days to cover a distance of over 78,000 km. The flame reached Africa and South America for the first time during this tour.

Can the flame go off during transit?

A common question regarding the Olympic flame is whether the flame can go off in transit, and if that happens does it mean that the entire process should begin again. It would be interesting to see what might happen if the Olympic flame would go out during a global tour at 77 thousand kilometres out of the 78 thousand.

Luckily for the people transporting the flame, they would not have to start all over again in Greece. The torch is allowed to go off, and in fact, this has happened on numerous occasions.

For example, during the Chinese Olympics, the flame had to be put out twice when passing through the UK after protesters came out to speak out against China's human rights abuses.

This event led to the IOC declaring in 2009 that the flame would only ever be relayed in the host country of the Olympics. This would prevent regions with differing political interests from engaging in hostilities.

It's worth noting that when the torch is re-lit, the fire used to light it is always from a backup fire lit using the Olympian fire in Greece.

A little fun titbit about the Olympic fire is that in 1976, the fire at the Olympic Games Quebec went out due to a rainstorm. One of the officials re-lit the fire using a cigarette lighter. Another official quickly put out the fire and informed the first official that this was against protocol. The fire was then re-lit using a backup from the original fire source.

Gymnastics As A Part of The Games

Gymnastics have been a part of the Olympics since its inception in the modern era. Gymnastics, however, was considered a secondary sport in the beginning, and it would be many years before gymnastics became the main performance of the games rather than a periphery distraction. Unfortunately for women, it wasn't until 1928 that they even were allowed to participate in gymnastic events.

The 1896 games in Athens

The inaugural games of the summer Olympics in 1896 were attended by over 280 athletes, all of whom were male. They came from a couple of countries and participated in games such as swimming, weight lifting, wrestling, fencing, shooting, and tennis. Gymnastics was a part of the games, but only men could participate in the games, like in all other sporting activities at the time.

A festive atmosphere prevailed at the games, and everyone knew that history was being made and reawakened in their presence as parades and banquets were held to mark the occasion. Members of the royal family of Greece helped organize and promote the event, which helped strengthen the event's prestige.

The organizers of the 1896 Olympic gymnastics were the Sub-Committee for Wrestling and Gymnastics. The gymnastics games took place from April 9th to 11th. There were 71 competitors from 9 different countries, with Greece overrepresented due to the Greek 51 gymnasts participating in the games.

The games in the competition included the team parallel bars, team horizontal bars, vault, pommel horse, rings, and rope climbing. The participating countries in the first games were Bulgaria, Hungary, Denmark, France, Germany, Great Britain, Greece, Sweden, and Switzerland.

The 1896 gymnastics medal table

Rank	Nation	Gold	Silver	Bronze	Total
1	Germany	5	3	2	10
2	Greece	2	2	2	6
3	Switzerland	1	2	0	3
Totals		8	7	4	19

The 1900 games in Paris

The second Olympic Games held were not in Greece but rather in France. This was done in part to attract people from other parts of the world. The belief was that if the games were held in other countries instead of only Greece, it would help bolster attendance by athletes from different parts of the world.

The second reason that the games were held in Paris was that this was the hometown of Pierre, baron de Coubertin, the founder of the modern Olympics and president of the International Olympic Committee (IOC).

It's important to remember that at this point of its development, the games were still a privately run affair. Despite the help of the Greek royal family, the Olympics were organized by private individuals and not the government. When the games were held in Paris, Pierre de Coubertin was disappointed to learn that the French government would bulldoze its way into taking control of the games.

The games turned into a disaster due to poor organization, small venues that couldn't fit crowds, and poor marketing, resulting in poor foreign spectator attendance. To make matters worse, the games were held for five months, resulting in a lack of interest from the masses.

The track and field events were terrible due to wet and uneven terrain, which was a risk for athletes. The swimming competitions happened in the Seine River, whose currents carried the swimmers at excessively fast paces, resulting in unrealistic finishing times. Few journalists attended the event, and the coordination was so poor that several officials and athletes didn't even know that they were participating in the Olympics.

The only two positive aspects of the French disaster were that the number of participating athletes from different countries increased, and women were allowed to participate for the first time. Of the 997 athletes in the games, there were 22 were women who competed in five sports, namely tennis, sailing, croquet, equestrianism, and golf.

The artistic individual all-around gymnastics results of Paris 1900

Rank	Gymnast	Nation	Score
1	Gustavo Sandras	France	302
2	Noel Bas	France	295
3	Lucien Demanet	France	293

The 1904 games in St. Louis

The next time the games were held was in St. Louis, USA.

After the Paris disappointment, many folks were hopeful that the American games would be better organised. The games were originally supposed to be held in Chicago, but the Olympics committee made the catastrophic mistake of moving them to St. Louis after they allowed themselves to be convinced that it would be a good idea to merge the games with the Louisiana exhibition that celebrated the acquisition of the territory.

The games were poorly marketed and poorly attended by foreign spectators and Americans. Political factors like the growing tensions that would lead to the Russo-Japanese war also kept people from sailing unnecessarily. Only 12 countries participated in the competition, a decline from the Paris games. There was also an interesting moment in which athlete Thomas Kiely arrived having financed his own travel rather than accepting to compete under the British flag, which highlighted the political tensions between Ireland and the UK.

In a gymnastics triathlon held, each competitor was required to perform a total of 9 routines, of which 3 were on each of the three separate apparatuses. The three routines included two compulsory exercises and one optional exercise.

Something to note about early gymnastics at the Olympics is that they contained many very rigorously challenging physical exercise –in other words, the competitions were more about physical strength than art or beauty.

The artistic individual all-around gymnastics results of 1904

Rank	Gymnast	Nation	Score
1	Julius Lenhart	Austria	69.80
2	Wilhelm Weber	Germany	69.10
3	Adolf spinier	Switzerland	67.99

The 1906 games in Athens

After the disappointments in Paris and St. Louis, the decision was made to return the games to Greece, which had already displayed the ability to host the games properly.

The games were not held in 1908, which would have been in line with the custom of holding the games after a break of four years, and as such, one might argue that these games weren't entirely legitimate. The games were referred to as the Intercalated Olympic Games.

Technicalities aside, the games attracted many athletes from Europe and America and resulted in the most competitive and exciting display of talent since the return of the Olympics in modern times.

Some Olympic historians have hypothesized that the Athens games probably saved the Olympics from an early demise. This is because the embarrassing fiascos of the Paris and St. Louis games had dampened people's spirits and attitudes. There was also talk that national games were better than international Olympic competitions.

Despite being the most important in modern times, it is worth noting that the Athens games are not actually included in the official IOC lists. The contention over whether to include the games was so hotly debated at the time and in years to come that the issue had to be revisited a century later when in 2004, the IOC read carefully through the petition to accept the games as official. After much deliberation, the board decided that they would not be official.

The success of the games in Athens led many people on the IOC boards to suggest that perhaps the games should be held only in Athens. In contrast, other members suggested that the games should be held in Athens once every two years but internationally once every four years.

London 1908 Olympic Games

The first time that the Olympic Games were held in London was a matter of luck. The games were actually supposed to be held in Rome, but due to financial problems, the decision was made to move the games to a country with the infrastructure to handle such a large event comfortably.

An all too common issue at the Olympics has always been that the games have often been used as a pulpit for people to air their political views. Many of these grievances were indeed legitimate, but this did not change the fact that they created a political atmosphere that sometimes overshadowed the games. That was the case when Finnish athletes protested the Russian government and the American athlete Rudolph Rose refused to dip the American flag to King Edward VIII. These incidences led to moments of awkwardness at the events.

The games were held at Shepherd's Bush Stadium, adding new events like diving, field hockey, motor boating, and indoor tennis. These additions helped to add to the flavour of the games. 12 nations participated in the games, and each team was allowed to produce 20 gymnasts for the events. France and Great Britain took advantage of this to enter the maximum number of gymnasts allowed, but other countries simply didn't have the manpower to do so.

The 1908 games were the third time when the men's individual all-around was a part of the competition. The first individual all-around competition was held in 1900, while the 1896 competitions only had individual apparatus events on the roster. The gymnastics competitions included the horizontal bar swinging movement, horizontal bar slow movements, parallel bars, rings swinging, rings stationary, pommel horse, and rope climbing.

The artistic individual all-around gymnastics results of 1908

Rank	Gymnast	Nation	Score
1	Alberto Braglia	Italy	317
2	Walter Tysol	GB	312
3	Loius Segura	France	297

Stockholm, Sweden, 1912

The Swedes had taken gymnastics more seriously than most other countries out there, and when they were chosen to host the games, they dedicated themselves to creating something truly magnificent.

The Swedes put up such a beautiful event that the media named it the *"Swedish masterpiece."* The 1912 games were well marketed, explaining why more than 28 countries participated. That was the highest participation rate in the history of the Olympics. The games also marked a major milestone for women who were included in the games like swimming, pentathlon, and diving.

One small problem with the games was when boxing was removed from part of the games that year. This was because the local community found the sport too rough and disagreeable. This angered the IOC, who decreed that local organizers would not have a say in which sports would be held in the future.

This time, the number of gymnasts allowed to each country was 6. This was a major reduction from the 20 during the 1908 games. A total of 9 countries participated in the event producing 44 gymnasts. Denmark and the Russian empire made their debut in the gymnastics category. This was the fourth time that the men's individual all-around was a part of the games.

Four of the top ten gymnasts in the 1908 games returned, and the question everyone was thinking about was whether Alberto Braglia of Italy would manage to defend his position as number one in the world. Sixth place Samuel Hodgetts of Great Britain was also a part of the games.

The artistic individual all-around gymnastics results of 1912

Rank	Gymnast	Nation	Pommel Horse	Rings	Parallel bars	Horizontal bars	Total
1	Alberto Braglia	Italy	34.75	31.75	34.75	32.75	135.00
2	Louis Segura	France	34.50	32.25	35.75	30.00	132.50
3	Adolfo Tunelsi	Italy	35.75	30.50	35.00	30.25	131.50

The 1920 games in Antwerp

There were no Olympic Games held in 1916 because of a world war. When the war ended, the defeated countries: Germany, Austria, Turkey, Hungary, and Bulgaria, were not allowed to attend. The Soviet Union voluntarily chose not to attend for political reasons.

The games were held in Belgium and were meant to help the world recover from the destruction of war, death, and devastation. This time, Alberto Braglia did not partake in the games since he had retired, choosing to go out while still on top. His career was one of the greatest in gymnastics history, having secured three medals. He suffered two tragedies; the first involved the loss of his four-year-old son, and the second was a major injury to his shoulder. These incidences led him to suffer depression before he could recover and continue with his career. When he eventually chose to retire, he became an acrobat who performed at circuses.

Egypt and Monaco made their Olympic debut at these games. Gymnasts had to partake in a compulsory and optional exercise in each of the rings, parallel bars and horizontal bar. Each gymnast was to perform a total of 8 exercises.

The event suffered from poor attendance because few people had the money to spend on tickets. Towards the end, the events were attended by school children who were given free attendance. A total of 2,600 athletes participated, of whom 60 were women. The Olympic flag was first introduced during these games.

The artistic individual all-around gymnastics results of Paris, 1920

Rank	Gymnast	Nation	Score
1	Giorgio Ziampori	Italy	88.35
2	Marco Torres	France	87.62
3	Jean Gounot	France	87.45

1924 Paris games

The 1924 games were an opportunity for Paris to show an improvement after their past debacle 24 years earlier. Paris was chosen as the centre of the games to honour Baron de Coubertin, who was retiring as head of IOC. That was an emotional tribute to a man who had dedicated his life to the success of the Olympic Games when few people in the world cared about them, and fewer still believed his goal was even achievable.

To the credit of the French, the games were a huge success. More than 100 women took part in the games, and fencing was added to the women's category. Tennis was dropped from the 1924 competition over questions regarding the amateur standing of the competitors, and it was not until 1988 that the sport was restored.

A total of nine events were contested at the gymnastics competition. Gold medallist Giorgio Ziampori returned to the competitions but, due to age, finished the competition at number 26.

National gymnastics rankings at the 2024 Olympics

Rank	Nation	Gold	Silver	Bronze	Total
1	Switzerland	2	2	3	7
2	Italy	2	0	1	3
3	Yugoslavia	2	0	0	2
4	Czechoslovakia	1	4	4	9
5	France	1	4	1	6
6	USA	1	0	0	1
Total		9	10	9	28

The 1928 Amsterdam Games

For women in gymnastics, the Olympics can only be said to have begun in 1928, with all preceding Olympic tournaments simply being practice runs before the main event. In the 1928 Amsterdam Games, the modern Olympics Games were born as women could finally be a part of the sport.

The discriminatory view that women couldn't handle the sport was disproven as women proved their metal and helped push gymnastics from a sideshow at the Olympics to a major part of the Games.

The performance of these women at the games convinced the International Association of Athletics Federations (IAAF) that women were capable of a high level of athletic performance.

What was the program like?

Each participating country had to offer a team of ten female gymnasts who would execute the following routines:

- 13-15 minutes: Either ensemble exercises: exercises with or those without portable hand apparatus, or exercises with as well as without portable hand apparatus

- 13-15 minutes: exercises involving the use of apparatus

- 9-10 minutes: vaults

- In total: 35-40 minutes

Each country was free to choose its composition of exercises, apparatus, and the exercises they would be executing.

The open-ended nature of the competition allowed each country to compete in the area that the female gymnasts were best at. However, this created a problem because it was difficult to compare and fairly judge various and different routines. How do you compare a routine involving flying rings with one on bars?

Sadly, there are no results for each individual performance, and all that remains are performances at a national level.

1928 drill women's competition

According to a Dutch newspaper that recorded the competition proceedings, the drill competitions were first. They began with a platform being placed in the middle of the field where the exercises would be conducted.

The Dutch ladies' team had a beautiful ensemble performance lasting about 13 minutes. The jurors awarded them 98.50 out of the possible 120 points. This already set an intimidating tone for the rest of the teams, who would have to try and match or surpass this.

A key thing to note about early competitions was that judges would award scores that varied widely from each other. The French drill score of 83.50 was composed of juror's points as follows 9, 12, 14.50, 15, 16.25, 16.75.

The judges had not yet adopted more homogenous and concise means of determining how to rate performances, hence the wide differences between the performances. The next performance was by the Italians, who matched the Dutch on the scales and the complete leg bend on 1 leg, which were perfectly executed. They got 92.75 because their performance wasn't quite as refined as the Dutch one.

The next team was the ladies of Great Britain dressed in scarlet tunics in a manner that looked out of the ordinary to the Dutch people. Their free exercises were a strong imitation of the Niels-Bukh method but not very well executed, so they only received 88.75.

The Hungarian team was fourth on the floor, and they stunned everyone by displaying a series of fast-paced exercises that were considered by many present to be the best that anyone had ever seen. They were awarded 99.25, which was higher than the Dutch.

The final team was the French. They managed to surpass every other team in terms of elegance. However, they couldn't match the gymnastic athleticism of other countries; thus, they got the lowest points at 83.50.

1928 women's Apparatus competition

According to the same 1928 Dutch article (which may be a little biased due to nationalist pride), the next phase of the competition involved apparatus. The Hungarian and French teams opted to go for lighter exercises, which proved insufficient to beat the gymnastic performances of the Dutch and Italians.

The Italian women's team used star balls, and their performance was quite good. The only downside was that they limited themselves to only one apparatus. The Dutch did not make this mistake because they used a low set of parallel bars, followed by a high set of parallel bars, ending with a turn on the rings. Nothing was too difficult; rather, the focus was on meticulous execution and avoiding unnecessary mistakes. They received 110 points out of possible 120 points. England got 94.50, France 84.50 and Hungary 78. With two parts of the gymnastics competition now accomplished, the

Netherlands led at 208.50 points. Italy was second at 194.75, England was third at 183.25, Hungary fourth with 177.25, and France was trailing at 168 points out of the possible 240 points.

The final results for women's gymnastics by country

Country	Drill	Apparatus	Vault	Total
1. Netherlands	98.50	110.00	108.25	316.75
2. Italy	92.75	102.00	94.25	289.00
3. Great Britain	88.75	94.50	75.00	258.25
4. Hungary	99.25	78.00	79.25	256.50
5. France	83.50	87.50	76.50	247.50

1932 Los Angeles, California, U.S.

The 1932 games couldn't have come at a worse time. The entire world had just gotten into the great depression, and most people were more interested in staying alive and not starving rather than sporting activities.

Only 1,300 athletes participated from 37 countries. This was the first time an Olympic village was organized, with most of the male participants staying in a suburb in Los Angeles named Baldwin. They had access to health facilities and recreational centres. Because they were fewer, the women stayed at a motel. The Los Angeles Coliseum was expanded so it could accommodate 100,000 visitors.

To make matters worse for the 1932 games, the International Federation of Gymnastics decided not to have women's gymnastics included as part of the competition despite its success in 1928.

1936 Berlin games

The Berlin Games have been a talked-about phenomenon for decades since they were held primarily because of where they were held. Three years after Adolph Hitler and the Nazi party had come to power, Berlin was hosting the games. There were many people around the world calling for the games to be boycotted due to the Nazi program of systematized racism. The charged political atmosphere only cooled down after a meeting was held by the IOC officials and German government officials. During the meeting, the government promised not to promote the Nazi ideology and to treat all athletes fairly regardless of their ethnicity. This was done officially; unofficially, newspapers used racial slurs to refer to black and Jewish athletes.

When the competitions commenced, the most talked-about victory was that of Jesse Owens. The black American athlete had amazed everyone with his skills at the games and put an end to Nazi pretensions of Aryan superiority.

As for the Gymnastics side of things, the 1936 program introduced compulsory routines to women. The ensemble routines entailed exercises that involved loosening the arms, legs, trunk as well as those involving the use of portable apparatus. The compulsory routine included the following: Balance Beam at 8 cm in width, uneven bar, and side horse vault without pommels

Results for gymnastics at the 1936 Summer Olympics – Women's artistic team all-around

Rank	Nation	Gymnast	Points
1 Gold	Germany	Käthe Sohnemann Julie Schmitt Paula Pöhlsen Trudi Meyer Anita Bärwirth Friedl Iby Isolde Frölian Erna Bürger	506.50
2 Silver	Czechoslovakia	Marie Větrovská Veřmiřovská Zdeňka Jaroslava Bajerová Matylda	503.60

		Pálfyová	
		Anna Hřebřinová	
		Vlasta Foltová	
		Božena Dobešová	
		Vlasta Děkanová	
3 Bronze	**Hungary**	Eszter Voi	499.00
		Judit Tóth	
		Olga Törös	
		Margit Nagy	
		Gabriella Mészáros	
		Ilona Madary	
		Margit Kalocsai	
		Margit Csillik	

8	Great Britain	Edna Gross	408.30
		Marion Wharton	
		Clarice Hanson	
		Brena Crowe	
		Doris Blake	
		Lilian Ridgewell	
		Mary Kelly	
		Mary Heaton	

The Berlin Games weren't just significant for their political tensions. They were also unique because that was the first time telex was used to transmit results. The telex system was the 1930s version of a telephone network used for two-way text-based messages. The Berlin games also had zeppelins used to quickly transport newsreel footage to other European cities. Zeppelins were airships filled with hydrogen, which is lighter than air, allowing them to fly great distances. These advancements in technology helped make the Olympic Games even more popular at an international level.

The 1948 London Olympic Games

As one might expect, just as World War 1 caused a temporary end to the Olympic Games, World War 2 also brought a similar fate. The games meant to be held in 1940 and 1944 were never held as the entire world was engulfed in the greatest war in human history.

As was the case in the past war, the defeated powers were not allowed to compete, so Japan and Germany had no athletes at the games. The German athletes always seem to get caught up on the wrong side of history.

This time, there was no Olympic village; instead, the men were housed in a military camp and at Uxbridge. The games attracted over 4,000 athletes from over 59 countries. There was poor weather which led to a sloppy display at the tracks. Wembley stadium was used for the opening ceremony and several aspects of the games.

As for women in gymnastics, this was the third time they would be performing at the games.

The results of the games were as follows:

Game	Gold	Silver	Bronze
Team all-round	Czechoslovakia	Hungary	USA
Individual-all round	Zdeňka Honsová Czechoslovakia	Edit Weckinger-Hungary Laura Micheli-Italy	
Vault	Karin Lindberg Sweden	Joan Airey-Great Britain Clara Schroth - United States	
Balance beam	Zdeňka Honsová Czechoslovakia	Irén Karcsics Hungary Miloslava Misáková-Czechoslovakia	
Flying ring	Zdeňka	Edit Weckinger	

	Honsová Czechoslovakia	- Hungary Laura Micheli - Italy	

Memorable Olympic Games Moments For Gymnastics

Since 1948, there have been many other tournaments held in which brilliant young women have gotten an opportunity to display their elegance, grace, strength, endurance, and ability to beat the odds in arenas historically thought to belong to men alone. It would be impossible to detail all the various tournaments, but it is possible to highlight some of the most memorable events for women's gymnastics at the Olympics.

Olga Korbut's crazy move

In 1972, Olga Korbut of the Soviet Union performed one of the most impressive manoeuvres in gymnastics history. Back then, the cold war was still hot, and the competition between the American athletes and Soviet athletes was a matter of propaganda for both governments. There was a lot of pressure on the athletes to prove who was better. Korbut had dazzled the fans at the games and the world by winning a gold medal in the beam and floor exercises. She had been favoured to win the all-round gold medal but actually ended up falling three times.

The highlight of her performance was that she was the first female athlete to perform a backward somersault on the balance beam. She executed it so perfectly that the move has been referred to as the "Korbut flip." Korbut was known for her beautiful smile at a time when Eastern Europe athletes were known to be cold and unemotional. Her charm and grace won over many Americans who were willing to set aside cold war rivalry to appreciate a truly amazing individual.

"Nadia Comaneci was Perfect in 1976"

Perhaps the most-talked-about moment in all of women's gymnastics was the performance by Nadia Comaneci in 1976. She is the only woman to ever achieve a perfect 10 out of 10 on the beam. The moment was so magical and surreal that the electronic board meant to show the score was not equipped to show a 10.00 score, so it just showed a 1.00 score.

The Romanian gymnast was so perfect in her performance that one journalist described her movements as swimming in the air. Her performance was flawless, and everyone agreed she deserved the ten score. She also helped her country secure a silver medal.

Nadia eventually grew tired of living under the misery of a communist dictatorship and defected from Romania at a time when such an attempt was punishable by death. She eventually settled in the United States and married another gymnast Bart Connor with whom she had a son.

1976 Shun Fujimoto performance

The 1976 Olympic Games were a pretty amazing tournament for gymnastics; they helped make the sport into what it is today. Nadia Comaneci wasn't the only gymnast to stun the world. Shun Fujimoto was equally impressive when he decided to continue with the games even after breaking his leg. The 26-year-old suffered a catastrophic leg injury while performing a floor exercise. Investigations revealed that he had broken the right kneecap. The Japanese team was in a tight race against the Soviet Union, and Fujimoto knew that if he dropped out, his team would lose. He scored a 9.5 on pommel horse with a broken knee and again ignored the pain to move the rings event.

Any sane person would say that trying ring manoeuvres with a broken knee isn't really possible, but the Japanese people are known for their iron resolve, and so he proceeded with the competition and achieved a career-best of 9.7. After such an outstanding performance, many joked that perhaps he should have been deliberately breaking his knee more often.

Kerri Strug in 1996

In 1996 Kerri Strug proved that women were just as capable of handling pain and pushing through it as men. Kerri withstood pain just like Shun Fujimoto had done 20 years earlier.

This feat was during the 1996 games. The American team had a 0.987 point lead over the Russian team to win the gold medal. This meant that the American team had to collapse to lose the medal. Unfortunately, this is exactly what started to happen as luck had turned against them, and everything that could go wrong was going wrong for them.

Entering the final vault, the first 4 Americans on the team all missed their landings. It didn't stop there; Dominique Moceanu then fell on all her attempts, and the only person on the team was Kerri Strug. Unfortunately, she was injured from previous performances and wasn't in any shape to execute a tough manoeuvre. To make matters worse, Russia's Roza Glieva still had a floor exercise to perform, so the Americans needed perfection if they were to win this.

Strug limped to the end of the runway and then made an obviously painful run towards the vault. She executed a Yurchenko entry vault, then leaped off the vault to land on the horse with her hands, and then pushed herself further into the air for an aerial double turn before landing on one leg. The pain was clear on her face, but she didn't let that stop her from staying composed. Her score was 9.712, and it was enough to get the USA their first team all-round gold medal. Strug had to be carried to the stage to receive her medal because she suffered a torn tendon and a third-degree lateral sprain. The fact she could walk, let alone perform such moves, was beyond a miracle.

Simone Biles wins big at the 2016 Olympics

If you asked any gymnast out there who she admires most, the answer you are likely going to get is Simone Biles. She won four gold medals at the world championships in 2014 in individual all-around, balance beam, and floor exercise events. She then won another four gold medals at the 2016 Olympics. Her victory at the Olympics made her a legend and a household name across America. By 2021, she had become the most decorated gymnast in world championship history.

The Olympic Games Versus The World Championships

A question that might come to mind is why the Olympic Games are far more known and prestigious than the world championships or the world cup. Many gymnasts who have won a medal or even reached the Olympics finals will often refer to this accomplishment ahead of any other.

The first thing to understand is that the world championships are held annually during non-Olympic years. Because they are held more often, their familiarity leads to a lower level of prestige.

Part of why the Olympics are more prestigious also has to do with perception. The Olympics have an air of mysticism about them as an ancient and glorious competition; they thus tend to carry greater weight.

Most gymnasts see the world championships as a means to prepare for the Olympics, and they use the opportunity to test their skills against the other world-class athletes to size up the competition. Sometimes gymnasts will even skip the world championships if they feel that it might interfere with their training routine too much as they prepare for the Olympics.

Where The Olympics Stand Today

It's strange that when the Olympics returned more than a century ago, most of the world was not really interested. It was seen as a hobby reserved for people filled with nostalgia for an ancient past.

Today, everything has changed as countries are willing to go to war with each other or bribe IOC officials for an opportunity to host the games in their country. Like most great things in life, the games started humbly and grew slowly into the giant they are today. More than three billion people worldwide have watched at least some part of the Olympic Games from their homes.

Merely participating in the games is considered a matter of great accomplishment, and winning a medal will result in athletes instantaneously becoming national champions.

Equally impressive is the degree to which women have made progress in the games. In the beginning, no women could participate, and yet today, they form a core part of the games, and as far as gymnastics is concerned, women are actually the main event.

In the next chapters, we will look at the history of Great Britain's performances in Gymnastics at the Olympics. We will highlight the highs, the lows, and the lessons learned throughout the years. We will also take note of the greatest British Olympic Gymnasts to see what can be learned from them.

Chapter 3: GB Gymnastics in the Olympics Over The Years

"If you mess up, don't panic. There's always a solution to the problem, and learning from your mistakes is one of the most important lessons in life."

Beth Tweddle, Olympic and Commonwealth champion

Great Britain is extremely impressive when we look at historical world rankings for all sports performances at the summer Olympics. The first country on the list is the United States which has 2,692 medals, followed by the Soviet Union which stands at 1,010 medals, and then Great Britain comes in at number three with 919.

There is no doubt that Great Britain stands above the rest at the Olympics, but what about gymnastics in particular? Well, the results here are mixed with a couple of pretty impressive moments. Unfortunately, the country has not been able to completely assert the kind of dominance it has shown in other sports.

Great Britain's women's national artistic gymnastics team has made an appearance at the Olympics 13 times and won two bronze team medals. One medal was won in 1928, and the other at the Tokyo games held in 2021.

Great Britain's women's team made an appearance at the Olympic Games as soon as women were allowed to do so in 1928. Unfortunately, there are many knowledge gaps regarding the events there because the details were not properly recorded or stored. This knowledge gap is in part because a huge portion of the women's gymnastics routines had not yet captured the imaginations of the media or public. After an unexpected, stunning performance at the games, more people took an interest, and more information became available in future games.

The 1928 Team

We can try and celebrate a couple of the names who won bronze at the first gymnastics Games in 1928. We don't know much about them, but there is enough for us to have a rough picture of who they were and what drove them to greatness.

Doris Woods

Doris Woods was a member of the Northampton Polytechnic Institute, and she represented Great Britain as part of the first national women's gymnastics team. She played a role in helping the team place third in the all-around at the games. After the games, she became a judge for future gymnastics games, and she used her personal history in the game to judge performances in the sport from a woman's perspective.

We don't know much about her personal life other than that she kept her surname after marriage. Beyond these few known facts, this unsung hero remains a mystery.

Hilda Smith

Born in 1909, Hilda was one of the two inaugural British women's Olympic gymnastics squads at the Amsterdam Games in 1928. She was seven weeks shy of her 19th birthday when she won the bronze medal for her country.

Ada Smith

Born in 1903, Ada Smith was the second gymnast for the inaugural British women's Olympic gymnastics squad at the Amsterdam Games in 1928. She went into the Olympics after placing third at the National Championships, just beneath Annie Broadbent and Carrie pickles. When her career was over, she coached gymnasts at the Marsh Gymnasium.

Ethel Seymour

Born in 1897, Ethel was a member of the Northampton Polytechnic Institute (NPI), just like Doris Woods. During the 1925 National Championships, she finished third behind Dorothy Billson and Jessie Kite.

Annie Broadbent

She was born in 1908, and before the Olympics, she had finished second at the Northern Counties competition and was the outright winner of the Yorkshire title. She stayed active even after winning in 1928 and won her only individual national title in 1930.

Lucy Desmond

Born in 1899, Lucy had won the inaugural national women's team title in 1923, and she was third at the national championships behind Pickles. Nothing much is known about her after she helped her team win bronze at the 1928 Olympics.

Other Competitors who took part in the 1928 games include Margaret Hartley, Amy Jagger, Isobel Judd, Jessie Kite, and Marjorie Moreman.

Great Britain At The 1936 Women's Gymnastics Games

During the Berlin games of 1936, Great Britain sent the following amazing women to represent them: Doris Blake, Edna Gross, Mary Heaton, Brenda Crowe, Clarise Hanson,

Mary Kelly, Lilian Ridgewell, and Marion Wharton. Many of these women had been present at the 1928 games with the hopes that they could repeat their success. Unfortunately, the team could not replicate their success; they came in at number eight.

The winners of the games were the Germans, who had 506.50 points, followed by Czechoslovakia with 503.60 points, and Hungary with 499 points and bronze. The games ended with no British victories in individual or team gymnastic sports.

1948 Games in London

The 1948 games were held in London, so there was a lot of pressure on the British team to make sure they got some medals for the fans. The fans were not disappointed as Britain won the second medal in women's gymnastics after Artistic gymnast Joan Airey won silver in the vault competition.

Before the competition, Joan was barely known. And so, her victory of silver in the vault came as a pleasant surprise for many people. She was a Regent Street Gymnastics Club member and was lucky enough to have been coached by Lucy Desmond, the same Lucy who had won the 1928 bronze medal and put Great Britain on the map at the very first games.

Later on, she took on a male coach George Weedon whom she credited with helping her master her skills. Interestingly her granddaughter would later become an Olympian herself after being inspired by the accomplishments of her grandmother. Her granddaughter's name is Lindsey, and she was a triathlete and modern pentathlete.

The 1948 team all-round went to Czechoslovakia gold, Hungary silver, and USA bronze, so Great Britain lost out on this.

A little on Joan W Airey

As the only British winner of the gymnastics category, it would only be right to look at the life of Joan Airey. Joan was born on 6th April 1926. Joan was a member of the Regent Street Gymnastics Club. George Weedon, a fellow club member, spotted Airey's talent and realized she was capable of greatness, so he took her under his wing to mentor her.

While unexpected, her victory at the Olympics was very warmly greeted back home. She helped inspire many other young women to get into the sport, and no doubt set the stage for many future medals for Team GB.

The 1952 Games In Helsinki

The 1952 games were a rather disappointing year for Team GB gymnastics. There was no victory in either the men's or women's gymnastics category. At the end of the competition, the gymnastics category was completely dominated by the Soviet Union, with 9 gold medals, 11 silver medals, and 2 bronze medals for 22 total medals. The Swiss were second with 7 medals, and the Hungarians were third at 8 medals but lower on points.

Other sports didn't fare well either, as Great Britain ended up ranked at number 18 with only 11 medals. The Finnish people have sometimes referred to the Helsinki Games as the last real Olympics. That is because there was less commercialization of the sport and a greater emphasis on strong sportsmanship. Several Olympic Games after were marred with doping allegations on various teams, such as the Soviet Union, which lowered the sport's prestige.

The 1956 Games in Melbourne

The 1956 games were another disappointment for gymnastics for team GB. There were no medals for the country either in the men's or women's categories. The only consolation was that other sporting categories did far better than at the 1952 games. This led to a table ranking of 8 due to 8 gold medals, 7 silver medals, and 11 bronze medals.

The Great Drought

After 1948, the Women's British gymnastics team did not win a single medal for 64 years. It's not entirely clear why this happened. Some people have speculated that there was a general decline in interest in the sport during this period. Another theory is that centralization of training may have led to this decline.

For some time, the youngest and best gymnasts would go to train at the Lilleshall National Sports Centre, but this came to an end in the late 2000s as young talent would instead train at their local clubs and teams. The diversity created by this more decentralized training method may be what led to a resurgence in British gymnastics.

The 2012 London Olympics

The 2012 summer Olympics were held in London. The fact that the games were held on British soil might explain why this was the first time in decades that the gymnastics team got back on the medal table.

The women

The following names represented the British women's artistic team;

- Hannah Whelan aged 20, from Stockport
- Jennifer Pinches aged 18, from High Peak
- Imogen Cairns aged 23, from Bristol
- Elizabeth Tweddle aged 27, from Bunbury
- Rebecca Tunney aged 15, from Manchester

The women's all-round team could not secure a medal, but Elizabeth Tweddle managed to win bronze for her performance on the uneven bars.

Short biography of Elizabeth Tweddle

She was born in Johannesburg, South Africa, in 1985 before moving to Bunbury with her family. She tried out several different sports when she was young before finally settling on gymnastics as her passion. She completed a foundation degree with Liverpool University, all while continuing to perfect her gymnastics skills.

She has described herself as a staunch football fan and supporter of Chester FC. She won three gold medals and two bronze at the world championships, plus a total of six gold medals at the European championships.

Her success at the Olympics and the world championships was critical to the renaissance of British gymnastics at the beginning of the twenty-first century after a long period of decline.

British gymnastics owe her for her valiant efforts in restoring the nation's pride in gymnastics. After her retirement in 2013, she joined the dancing on ice TV series, where she came in third.

The men

The men's all-round team won bronze in the competition. Some controversy in the competition ensued when the judges awarded points to Japan's Kōhei Uchimura score for his pommel horse routine. It impacted the scoreboard such that it looked like England would lose out. The British team composed of;

- Sam Oldham
- Daniel Purvis
- Louis Smith
- Kristian Thomas

- Max Whitlock

The men's British team made their country proud by winning both silver and bronze for the pommel horse routine. The winners were Louis Smith and Max Whitlock.

Louis Smith was born in 1989, and this was not his first time winning an Olympic medal. He had already won bronze in the men's pommel horse in the 2008 Beijing Olympics before winning it again in 2012. He would win the medal again before he eventually retired.

Max Whitlock was born in 1993, and even before winning bronze at the Olympics, he had made a name for himself with victories at the world championship. He has won three gold medals and five silver medals at the world championships throughout his career.

At the end of the competition, Britain ranked 12th for one silver medal and three bronze medals for four medals. The competition's winner was China, with five gold medals, four silver, and three bronze.

The 2012 Olympics were a huge success in the gymnastics category and the entire competition. Great Britain ranked 3rd overall after the United States and China. Great Britain had 29 gold medals, 18 silver, and 18 bronze medals. This was the country's best performance in history.

The 2016 Olympic Games

The 2016 games held in Rio were an even greater success for the gymnastics team than the 2012 London games. The team's achievements really helped make Team GB worthy of respect and even a little fear from the other teams. The competitions were held at the Arena Olímpica do Rio, where 18 events were hosted involving 63 countries.

The British men's medallists included max Whitlock, who won gold for floor exercises, bronze for the individual all-round, and gold for the pommel horse. His impressive victories put Great Britain on the map and helped the country acquire a very respectable position on the gymnastics table. Louis Smith, Whitlock's teammate, also made his country proud by winning silver on the pommel horse, just behind his teammate.

The other winner in the men's category was Nile Wilson, who won bronze for the horizontal bar. He was born in 1996, and he had been a part of the silver medal-winning team at the world championships a year earlier.

At 25 years of age, he announced his retirement from competitive gymnastics in January 2021. In total, the men's gymnastics team won two gold medals, one silver, and two bronze medals for five medals.

Given the tremendous success of the men's team, this was a clear challenge to the women's team, which has traditionally been the stronger of the two sides. Meeting this challenge were two amazing gymnasts named Amy Tinkler and Bryony Page. Amy won bronze for floor exercise performance, while Page won bronze for the individual trampoline performance.

Amy Tinkler bio

Amy Tinkler was born in 1999 and hailed from Bishop Auckland, where she lived until moving to Essex after changing gyms. She competed at the 2013 British Artistic Championships, where she won second place. Tinkler took the Gold medal on the uneven bars with a score of 12.900.

Even before Amy Tinkler's success at the Olympics, she had already won gold at the British all-round competition, marking her debut as a senior competitor. While warming up for the Birmingham world cup, she tore a ligament that prevented her from competing for a while. She retired from professional gymnastics in 2020 at the age of 21.

An interesting fact about Amy is that she attended Durham High School for Girls, where she took her GCSEs for three years to accommodate her gymnastics training. This highlights a critical issue of how gymnastics training can affect the career of a young gymnast. The gymnastics career is usually over by a person's mid-twenties, with very few managing to keep at it professionally into their early 30s. Given this early retirement, many need to adopt a new career, so doing well in academics suddenly becomes important.

Bryony Page's bio

Page was born in December 1990 in Crewe but brought up in Wrenbury. She took up a trampoline at the tender age of nine. Early in her career, she suffered from the yips.

Having concluded a deep dive into women's British gymnastics history, we can now look at the events that transpired in preparation for the Tokyo 2020 Olympics games. This will be the focus of the next chapter.

Chapter 4: The Build-Up To The Tokyo 2020 Olympics

"Nothing is more expensive than a missed opportunity."

Jackson Brown

The process of choosing a city to host the Olympic Games is long and challenging. It involves jumping through one hoop after another, all in the hopes of pleasing a notoriously implacable Olympics committee that can choose to overlook you for the slightest issue.

Tokyo may have appeared the obvious choice to host the Olympics, but this was simply hindsight bias. The truth is that Tokyo had a couple of issues perceived as weaknesses that could be exploited by other cities hoping for the privilege of hosting the tournament. So let's begin by looking at the Tokyo bidding process.

The Japanese Bid

No one can deny that there is great honour and prestige in hosting the Olympics. That is why so many countries work both in public and behind the scenes to make sure that their bids for hosting the Olympic Games are taken seriously.

To be clear, the Olympic Games aren't just about prestige. However, like most things in life, they also have a lot to do with money. The games draw in thousands of tourists to the host country, who spend millions in the country. The revenue bump gotten from this influx of tourists more than makes up for the costs associated with hosting the tournament.

The process of selecting a city to host the 2020 games began way back in 2011. The National Olympics Committee was considering six cities: Istanbul, Baku, Tokyo, Madrid, Rome, and Doha.

Phase one is referred to as the Candidature Acceptance Procedure. At this stage, the International Olympics Committee performs a preliminary review of each city's ability to host the event. This is important because the Olympics draw in tens of thousands of people from all over the world. The host city must have an airport capable of handling the additional traffic and the accommodations for all these new visitors. The transportation system has to be able to handle the additional traffic on the roads and trains, or else there will be severe congestion. These are just a few of the factors that the committee looks into.

Luckily for the five of the six cities, Italy dropped out of the bidding process while still at stage one. The Olympics issue had become a point of massive political tension because many Italians criticized the government for daring to spend additional money when their budget was already so strained.

The committee asked the remaining cities to respond to a questionnaire that required cities to offer information critical to determining their capacity to host the event. The answers were then submitted in what is called an applicant file. These answers were reviewed, and three cities were chosen to move on to the next phase. These cities were Tokyo, Istanbul, and Madrid.

In phase two, the three remaining cities were required to provide an in-depth analysis of exactly how they planned to host the event should they win the bid. They were then expected to prepare for a visit by the evaluation committee, who would physically inspect the most relevant issues concerning hosting the event. The evaluation committee would want to see the infrastructure for themselves to determine if the respective city was capable of hosting such an event.

The evaluation commission visited Tokyo from 4-7 March 2013, Madrid from 18-21 March 2013, and Istanbul from 24-27 March 2013. Following the visits, the evaluation committee made a technical appraisal of each city's ability to host the event. The report was then made public and distributed to the IOC members. This is done to ensure no favouritism in assessing the different cities.

A technical briefing meeting was then held over two days from 3-4 July 2013. This gave the IOC members a chance to discuss the technical elements of the three bids. The culmination of the bidding process came in September 2013 in Buenos Ares during the 125th IOC session. Each city had 45 minutes to present a presentation on why they deserved to win the bid and 15 minutes to answer questions. After the presentations, the Chair of the evaluation committee, Sir Craig Reedie, addressed the session, after which the IOC members proceeded to vote on which city should win the bid.

The eligible IOC members could only vote once in each round of voting. IOC members who are citizens of the countries participating in the bidding process could not vote. In round one of voting, Istanbul got 26 votes, Madrid got 26 votes, and Tokyo got 42 votes.

Under normal circumstances, the city that receives the fewest votes gets automatically removed from the bidding process. However, this year was unique because both Madrid and Istanbul tied at 26 votes each. That meant the next voting stage couldn't take place until a tie-breaker vote could be held. The tie-breaker vote was held, and the result was 49 votes for Istanbul and 45 votes for Madrid.

The second and final round of voting proceeded, but as many people expected, the clear winner of the voting process turned out to be Tokyo. The truth is that even before the voting process had commenced, there had been leaks from inside the IOC stating that Tokyo was the favourite to win the bidding process on the condition that they didn't make any major mistakes. Based on technical grounds alone, Tokyo was clearly the best city to host the tournament, and so when two anonymous sources leaked that they were going to win, there wasn't much of a surprise.

Madrid and Istanbul had held out any hopes that Tokyo would lose on the bid because Japan had experienced an earthquake in 2011, resulting in radioactive leakage into the atmosphere from the Fukushima nuclear power plant. Many potential visitors from across the world were still very wary of going to Japan and being exposed to radiation that could lead to cancer and other health problems.

As various media outlets started covering this risk, what was supposed to be a slam dunk for Japan suddenly looked uncertain and potentially doomed. For this reason, Prime Minister Shinzo Abe personally flew to go and speak to the IOC and reassure them that the Fukushima situation was contained and there was no risk to the health of visitors.

When Tokyo was announced as the winner, there was an uproar of Joy and tears within the Tokyo delegation. As for Madrid and Istanbul, the despair was clear to see. Spanish tennis player Feliciano Lopez was furious and vented his anger at the IOC by stating that they had no regard for fair play and failed to consider the interests of all sports involved in the competition.

On their part, the Turks were angry that their vision for uniting both East and West as a nexus of different civilizations and cultures had failed. Despite the rage of the Istanbul delegation, various pundits concluded that the decision to overlook Istanbul was because while the infrastructure in the city was capable of handling the various sports and traffic, the city just wasn't pretty enough for the high standards set by the IOC. Another factor that came into play was accusations of doping among Turkish athletes, which contributed to a negative image.

The Emergence Of COVID-19

As humans, we all have limited time on this planet. Therefore, nature compels us to ensure that we take advantage of this limited time to accomplish our heart's desires before it is too late.

For athletes engaged in different sports fields, this fact is not just a matter of urgency; it is also a high-degree imperative. That is because athletes rely on the strength and vigour of their bodies. This vigour declines with age, and at a certain point, the body simply can't keep up with the challenges brought up by the struggle.

The situation is even worse for gymnasts because while most sports have competitors retiring in the early to mid-thirties, this is not the case for gymnasts. The strenuous nature of the sport means that most gymnasts have to retire by their mid-twenties. Because of this fact, many gymnasts understand that they have to take advantage of their physical fitness while they still can. Any missed opportunity to compete in a major international competition is a huge blow to a gymnast's career.

With these facts in mind, it is important to remember that the Olympic Games play out once every four years. Because of this, many gymnasts focus all their training and emotional energy on preparing for the Olympics, knowing that this could be the most important moment of their lives. The sheer dedication, sweat, and tears that go into preparing for this event cannot be articulated in words. It can only be fully appreciated by watching the heartbreak felt by Olympians when they crash out of the competition. Nobody could have foreseen that a global pandemic would emerge and completely upset the entire world, including the 2020 Tokyo Olympic Games.

In early 2020, the emergence of a strange new virus in China was largely ignored not only by experts but also by the sporting world. Nobody could have imagined that the strange disease, then commonly called coronavirus, would upend the entire community and the entirety of human civilization.

There was an endless barrage of jokes about the virus, and most people simply went on with their lives as normal. Every potential Olympian was focused on training for the Tokyo Olympics, which was destined to be the year's biggest event outside the political arena.

The Japanese were absolutely ecstatic about the event. The Japanese bid to host the event had been a long and arduous road. So when it became increasingly clear that the coronavirus outbreak was going to be a major issue in 2020, the Japanese started paying attention.

The first major reports of an outbreak of coronavirus were in late 2019 in Wuhan, China. It wasn't until February 2020 that Japan had a major coronavirus outbreak when Diamond Princess Cruise Ship developed cases. The ship was British-owned, but the outbreak emerged after a man who had flown to Tokyo from Hong Kong Boarded the ship while infected. The infection quickly spread throughout the ship. There were 2,666 passengers on the ship, of whom 712 were confirmed to have the virus, and approximately 7-14 died from the condition.

At the beginning of the outbreak in Japan, the head of the Tokyo 2020 Olympics organizing committee Toshiro Muto stated that the committee was keeping an eye on the development of the pandemic. Still, there would be no cancellation of the event. His exact words in early February were, "I am seriously worried that the spread of the infectious disease could throw cold water on the momentum towards the Games." Toshiro stated that he hoped that the disease would be stamped out completely as soon as possible. These concerns were also echoed by the mayor of the Olympic village, where 11,000 athletes were expected to be staying. Mayor Saburo Kawabuchi stated that he hoped that the infections would end or else operating the Olympics would not be a smooth endeavour.

At this point in the disease's development, there had been no deaths in Japan, but they had the highest infection rate outside of China. As the disease would progress over the next month, it became increasingly clear that the hopes of Mr. Toshiro and Mayor Saburo would not pan out. The disease continued to spread worldwide, and death rates increased each passing week. A month later, Canada became the first country to pull out of the Olympic Games over concerns that their athletes would not be safe during the games and would return to Canada infected.

The preliminary qualification games were postponed or moved to different locations as concerns grew. An example of this was the women's basketball qualification games that were moved from Asia to Belgrade in Serbia. Other qualification games were moved to Jordan, France, and the UK.

As the situation continued to worsen, it became increasingly obvious that the games would have to be postponed, and the only question was to what date they should be postponed to. Japanese Prime Minister Shinzo Abe, who had so diligently worked to get the games hosted in his country, was now in a tough spot. He could either push on with the games and risk several countries failing to attend or push them to a later date and hope that things would calm down.

The problem with postponement was that a huge cost was incurred in getting the necessary infrastructure in place for the games. Any postponement would mean additional costs. The prime minister said it was okay to postpone the games for a maximum of one year. The national institute of health estimated that states of emergency would have to be declared if the games were held, and more than 10,000 cases would emerge if the games went ahead.

With all these factors weighing in, the decision was made to postpone the games by one year to the next summer. Instead of the games being held from 24th July to 9th August 2020, they would be held from 28th July to 8th August 2021.

Short Biographies of Participating British Gymnasts

"Being selected to represent your country at an Olympic Games is an outstanding achievement. All four athletes should be exceptionally proud of what they have achieved, and I am sure they will relish everything that this opportunity brings."

These are the words of Mark England, the Team GB Chef de Mission for the Tokyo Games. He spoke these words to refer to the four female athletes who had succeeded in becoming the representatives of their country at the games. The four female athletes were Alice Kinsella, Amelie Morgan, and the twin sisters Jennifer Gadirova and Jessica Gadirova.

Alice Kinsella

Alice was born in Essex but raised in the midlands. She stands at 5 feet and 3 inches. She has green eyes, brunette hair, and –for the more superstitious reader– is a Pisces.

Alice comes from a "sporty family" as her father was a professional footballer who played for Ireland in several international games, including the world cup in 2002. Alice's older brother, Liam, is a midfielder for league two-side team Walsall. Alice believes she has had it rougher because "gymnastics is harder than football: "... they are just kicking a ball around whereas we are doing no-handed flips on a four-inch beam."

Her parents, Mark and Karen, took Alice to the Telford's Wrekin Gymnastics Club when she was seven years old. It was here that fate had determined that the budding gymnasts would meet her gymnastics coach Christine Still. As a coach, Christine has been known to have high expectations. And so, upon meeting Alice's parents, she was quick to inform them not to expect too much from their daughter because even the best gymnasts lose some of the time. Alice's father was quick to agree with this fact because, as a footballer, he understood losing was a part of the game.

Over time, they both understood that while they both focused on managing expectations, Alice had focused on surpassing all expectations. After just one season of training, the now eight-year-old Alice had become the regional and national champion for her age group. According to her coach, her victory was because she possessed two critical requirements for success in gymnastics: speed and coordination.

Things weren't always easy for Alice. At around age 12, she competed in England's School Games. By this time, she had already grown accustomed to the stability provided by Park Wrekin Gymnastics Club. So when a new revolving door of coaches was introduced into her life, she struggled to cope with the changes. It takes time to acclimate to the tempo, attitude, style, and expectations of a new coach, and so when coaches are changing at a fast pace, there can be challenges with readjusting.

During the 2008 Olympics, Alice was still training nearly every moment she was free and even missed a few classes to hone in on her skills. The 2008 games had a huge emotional impact on Alice, and the entire experience of watching the best gymnasts in the world only hardened her resolve to work even harder. The achievements of Russian-born American gymnast Nastia Liukin were particularly interesting to Alice.

"She was one of my idols," Alice explained and watching her performance made her dream bigger.

As Alice grew older, she started to generate faith from her coaches, who believed she could have Olympic success one day. This hope was derailed when at the age of 14-15, she failed to make it to the top of the pyramid for the junior team for European competitions. Alice used this disappointment to drive her toward greater heights. One year later, she succeeded in making it to the European competitions and winning two medals against the best in Europe. This victory put her name on everyone's lips as they realised she would be a force to reckon with in the future.

After this victory, Coach Still sat down with Alice and her mother and informed the young athlete that she could receive funding from the National Lottery fund. This would allow her to focus more of her attention on gymnastics. It also meant that this would be her future career, and all eyes would be on her to succeed to ensure public funds do not go to waste. Alice didn't bother thinking much about it because she immediately said her answer was yes. She was certain about what she wanted to do with her life and ready to make a major commitment. As Coach Still put it, this was the moment "when it became clear she'd move towards gymnastics as a career."

In 2017, Alice's senior debut was at the Stuttgart world cup, where she finished seventh in ranking. She also participated in the Artistic Gymnastics Championships in Romania, where she took the tenth place in the all-round. While not winning any medals, this was still a good start for the now-adult athlete.

In 2018, Alice stunned everyone with an exceptional performance at the Commonwealth Games, winning the all-round bronze medal. She then went on to become the 2019 European champion for the balance beam, which was the biggest moment of her career until then. As she described it when she was named champion *"I was so nervous watching the rest of the girls compete and to come away with our first ever European beam medal feels absolutely amazing."*

Jennifer Gadirova

If there has ever been a case for genes playing a part in athletic success, the amazing pair of twins, Jennifer and Jessica, would have to be the poster children. The two sisters resemble each other almost to a T, and when they stand next to each other, no one will fault you for mistaking one twin for the other.

Jennifer was born on 3rd October 2004 in Dublin, Ireland, after her father, Natig Gadirova, had moved to the region for work-related reasons. Jennifer maintains dual citizenship in Ireland and Great Britain. Her height is 5 feet and 6 inches, and she has brown hair and brown eyes.

Jennifer was brought up in Aylesbury, Buckinghamshire, and started gymnastics at age 6. Many people who go into gymnastics tend to have been engaged in a related field beforehand, like dancing. That was not the case for Jenifer, who had to rely solely on her instincts and natural talent. Jennifer would dedicate 30 hours a week to training and perfecting her skills. According to Jennifer, both sisters attempted various other sports at their mother's request. However, it soon became clear that they clicked perfectly with gymnastics.

Like many other gymnasts her age, Jennifer's personal hero is US artistic gymnast Simone Biles. In 2016, she ranked 4th in the Christine Bowker artistry trophy. This went on to put her name on people's lips as a potential future star. In 2018, would take the 12th place in the English championships and 6th on the vault.

In 2019, she again participated in the English championships, and this time won the gold medal on the floor, silver on the vault, and bronze on uneven bars.

Both Jennifer and her sister were eager to participate in the Tokyo Olympics. Her sister Jessica was the first to receive the glorious news of being chosen to participate in the competition. The two girls had to wait another 20 minutes before Jennifer received the news that she had also been chosen to represent her country. This was important to them because they had been working hard together for several years. If only one of them had made it, it would have been disappointing. Each twin considers the other's success as their own, and they really are two peas in a pod.

To quote Jennifer herself, "I heard her news, and I was so happy, but then, like, I don't want to get my hopes up - would I get in? But then, as soon as I had the phone call, I was just like, we've done it together."

Their close friendship and bond doesn't mean that they always spend time together. Like everyone else in the world, they too need alone time to think and develop their unique personalities. As Jennifer put it, "We do spend every second with each other. But I feel like sometimes we do need that independence from each other and just focus on ourselves without her always being right by my side. We are individuals at the end of the day, so we do enjoy having our time apart but not if it's too long until we see each other again."

It's easy to see why Jennifer had such tremendous success at such a young age. Her dedication and relentless pursuit of her goals set her apart from many other girls in her age group who see gymnastics simply as a hobby. Jennifer's personal motto is *"Think big, trust yourself and make it happen."* She lives by these words, and it is clear that she has a brilliant career ahead of her.

A final thing to note about Jennifer is her warm and approachable personality, encapsulated in her naïve yet captivating smile. She is almost always happy, which makes it easier for her to relate with her coaches and fans.

Jessica Gadirova

Jessica Gadirova is a mirror image of her sister, Jennifer. They share a similar height, hair colour, and warm smile. Having a sister who understands all the challenges associated with the sport of gymnastics and can have your back for emotional support at moments when other family members aren't typically allowed has been a huge boost for the twins. This doesn't mean that everything has been perfect or rosy.

Anytime siblings compete in the same sport, there is always the added tension of the public making comparisons between the two. For example, the constant comparisons between Serena and Venus Williams were the staple of sports magazines and pundit talk. This pressure creates an emotional roller-coaster where a touch of emotional sibling rivalry emerges, which goes hand in hand with feelings of disappointment each time one sibling has a difficult time on the floor. Jessica and Jennifer seem to have managed this problem well because they are always ecstatic about each other's success.

Even before the Olympics, Jessica had a pretty good career. In 2016, Gadirova was placed the 12th all round after competing at the British Espoir Championships. She would take the 6th place on the balance beam where it was a tie. In March 2018, she competed at the British championships and placed 7th in the all-round and 8th in the uneven beams.

In March 2019, Jessica again competed at the English Championships and placed fourth behind Ondine Achampong, Halle Hilton, and her sister Jennifer.

Amelie Morgan

Amelie Morgan was born on 31st May 2003 in Slough, Berkshire. In a twist of fate, Amelie, just like Jessica and Jennifer Gadirova, also has a twin sibling, and he practices gymnastics too.

Amelie started her gymnastics career in 2008 at Chiltern Gymnastics, located in Iver. Later she joined the Slough Gymnastics club in 2010 as soon as it opened. She worked pretty hard by putting in 35 hours into training every week.

Amelie's first major competition was in 2015 when she competed in the English championships and came out second at the Espoir level. She took part in school games competition in 2016, where she took the third place in the all-round. She then competed at the Olympic hopes cup (not to be confused with the Olympic Games), and she placed second in the all-round just behind Ana Padurariu of Canada.

Many prestigious schools often approach really talented gymnasts like Amelie to join their programs. In 2017, she announced she was in talks with UC Berkley to join their school on a scholarship. In the end, she decided not to pursue that opportunity and instead joined the University of Utah. She would later compete at the European Youth Olympic Festival, where she won bronze on the balance beam.

In 2018 she again competed in the British and English championships, winning gold in both competitions. She was chosen to represent Great Britain in the 2018 European championships, and she won a record five medals while there.

A string of injuries

Perhaps the greatest challenge that Amelie has had to face was a string of injuries that began in 2019. Amelie sustained an injury just after the European championships but was lucky enough to heal before the 2019 world championship. The injury forced the team to place her in a reserve position for the Stuttgart games because she reinjured herself, and Kelly Simmons, a fellow gymnast, took her place.

She worked on getting better, and in 2020, she announced that she would take part in the American cup taking place on March 7. Unfortunately, she was injured again, and Jennifer Gadirova took her position.

As with any other sport, injuries can have a huge impact on the health and fitness of a gymnast. There were a lot of questions emerging as to whether she would be able to take part in the Olympic Games. In the end, Amelie was named as part of the team that would represent Great Britain and only time would tell if this was the right call or not.

Getting Close to The Big Date

The Olympic Games had been postponed by one year due to the COVID-19 pandemic. Unfortunately, one year later, the disease was still around and a potential threat to the games. Athletes worldwide were getting tired of the wait because each year that passed by was an opportunity to take advantage of the fact that their bodies were still fit enough to partake in the games. As such, nobody was interested in any further delays regardless of the risks.

The governors of Tokyo and Osaka were still extremely cautious weeks before the opening of the games. They even requested that the Central government extend the state of emergency to deal with the fourth wave. Under these measures, large commercial malls were barred from operating, alcohol-serving establishments would be closed, and residents were advised to abstain from unnecessary outings.

The Olympic committee stated that regardless of the situation on the ground, the games would continue. The Japanese government agreed, and all that remained was ironing out the details. The union of Japanese doctors was still calling for a stop to the games, but the government insisted that the costs would be too high.

The government announced that foreign visitors would not be allowed to travel to see the games, but 10,000 domestic fans would be allowed into the venues to watch the games. Additionally, the fans were expected to maintain safety rules to prevent an outbreak. The committee decided to use artificial sounds that mimic large crowds at the stadium to avoid the awkward sound of empty or barely filled pitches. Days before the opening ceremony, the WHO chief supported the opening of the games because of the precautions taken, so the games were now clear to begin.

Chapter 5: The Tokyo 2020 Olympics Experience And Final Scores

"I don't run away from a challenge because I am afraid. Instead, I run toward it because the only way to escape fear is to trample it beneath your feet."

Nadia Comaneci

After the COVID-19 chaos of 2020 and the postponement of the summer Olympics to 2021, there was a palpable eagerness in the atmosphere. Team GB would be taking part in a huge array of competitions ranging from swimming and cycling to Judo and shooting. A couple of winners in the previous Olympic games were here to defend their medals against impossible odds, while various newbies were hoping to make their mark for the first time.

The favourites to win the competition were the Americans because they had won the 2016 Rio Olympics by a significant eight points. This was largely due to the efforts of Simone Biles, who had racked up 4 gold medals at the competition. The obvious American dominance didn't deter other major challengers like the Chinese and Team GB from believing they too could emerge on top.

COVID-19 Health Measures

Part of the reason governments worldwide allowed their gymnasts to travel for the Tokyo Games were the health safety measures put in place by the IOC and the Japanese government.

These measures included All game participants, regardless of whether they were athletes, coaches, or fans, would be required to undergo two COVID-19 tests before traveling to Japan for the games. Any individual with a positive test or showing symptoms would not be allowed to attend the games. Temperatures were taken each time athletes went into the Olympics village. COVID-19 tests were necessary whenever an individual was in an area with a large group of people. Attendees were advised to get vaccinated, and quarantine was necessary for three days after arriving in Japan. Spectators were banned from lining the route of the Olympic marathon, and in instances where fans were allowed to attend the games, they had to maintain social distancing.

Qualifier Rounds

Before proceeding to the finals, the various teams and individuals must first defeat several rivals in the qualifier rounds. Here is how the qualifiers work:

A dozen nations will compete for the team titles, and they are grouped into five sub-divisions.

Women's artistic individual all-around qualifiers

The Women's qualification rounds for individual all-round took place on 25th July 2021. There were a total of 39 competitors in this qualification round. Team GB was part of the games with Amelie Morgan, Alice Kinsella, Jessica Gadirova, and Jennifer Gadirova representing the country. The person to beat was Simone Biles, who everyone expected would top the qualification rounds.

Results of the artistic individual all-round qualifiers

Only the top 20 scoring gymnasts progressed onto the AA finals. The twins Jessica and Jennifer made it to the finals in 12th and 17th place in the individual all-rounds. Unfortunately, Amelie Morgan and Alice Kinsella could not reach the finals, having finished in 33rd position and 48th position respectively. Having two candidates in the finals was pretty good for Team GB. Only the Americans, Italians, and French had two athletes in the finals.

Unfortunately, Alice Kinsella had a rough qualification round. After suffering an ankle injury in the days leading up to the competition she was not in peak physical condition. Her stronger pieces were bars and beam, which she had some major mistakes on.

Although she had won in the qualifier rounds, Simone Biles had announced she would not be competing in the finals for mental health reasons. Her mental health issues had to do with two issues. The first was that she was anxious about getting injured. In a later interview, she would state; *"I'm going home in one piece, which I was a little bit nervous about"* The second problem was that she was suffering from a serious case of the twisties, also known as the yips or a mental block (we shall discuss this condition a bit more later).

Simone getting out of the competition was lucky for the other athletes. However, it raised very serious concerns regarding the question of whether Olympics officials, coaches, and parents are actually looking into the emotional well-being of their athletes.

The all-round qualifier includes the following categories, vault, uneven bars, balance beam, and floor exercises. It's not really possible to discuss all the gymnasts' performances. Thus, this chapter will only highlight the really impressive performances.

British Gymnastics at The Olympics

Rank	Name	Country	Vault	Uneven bars	Balance beam	Floor	Total
1	Simone Biles	USA	14.966	14.566	14.066	14.133	57.731
2	Rebecca Andrade	Brazil	15.400	14.200	13.733	14.066	57.399
3	Sunisa Lee	USA	14.333	15.200	14.200	13.433	57.166
4	Angelina Melnikova	ROC	14.466	14.933	13.733	14.000	57.0132
5	Vladislva Urazova	ROC	14.600	14.866	14.000	13.633	57.099
6	Victoria	ROC	14.300	14.766	13.866	14.000	56.932

	Listunova						
7	Nina Derwael	Belgium	13.900	15.366	13.766	13.566	56.598
8	Tang Xinjing	China	14.300	14.333	14.433	13.366	56.432
12	Jessica Gadirova	GB	14.500	13.800	12.866	14.033	55.199
17	Jennifer Gadirova	GB	14.533	13.066	13.300	13.800	54.699
33	Amelie Morgan	GB	13.858	13.833	13.033	12.466	53.190

Simone Biles on the vault

On her first attempt on the vault Simone biles performed a very difficult vault with a massive D score of 6.00 known as 'The Cheng' as it was first performed by a Chinese gymnast

Cheng Fei in 2005 The vault had a yurchenco entry with a half on, and 1.5 twisting layout. However, it was clear to everyone that this was not her best performance. This was primarily because she made a mistake referred to as being "high on the table." This happens when an athlete jumps too hard on the bottom floor spring, and jumps so high that her hands can't apply enough pressure on the second spring. This creates an inability to execute a sufficient number of turns while in the air. Her landing was also not good as she took a large step on landing outside of the landing area incurring a 0.3 penalty . Her first vault gave a score of 14.966.

Simone Biles first vault results

Name	Difficulty	Execution	Penalty	Total
Simone Biles	6.000	9.266	0.30	14.966

Jessica Gadirova on the vault

As for Jessica Gadirova, she started with a powerful run and then executed a yurchencko entry vault with a double twisting somersault. Her performance was neat and tidy, but would have been deducted for a small step, and her chest was a little low on landing.

Name	Difficulty	Score
Jessica Gadirova	5.4	14.533

Jennifer Gadirova on the vault

Similarly to her sister Jennifer also executed a double twisting yurchencko. She displayed a lovely flight phase, but took a large step on landing, which would have incurred some deductions.

Name	Difficulty	Score
Jennifer Gadirova	5.4	14.533

Amelie Morgan on the vault

After a powerful run, Amelie did a round-off yurchenkco entry onto the vault before pushing herself off the horse and executing a single twist in the air. Her landing and overall execution were good, but the performance was not as difficult meaning a lower E score.

Name	Score
Amelie Morgan	13.858

Jennifer Gadirova on the beam

She mounted the beam with a backwards aerial flip, landing on the beam with her chest in what is called the candle stick position. She lifted herself up and executed a few dance skills on the beam, and stood on the edge. She performed her leap series which was a change leg split leap, change leg split leap with half turn into a back tuck somersault. There was a slight delay in the connection ot this series, which might not have given her the bonus point connections from the judges. Her acrobatic series was performed with confidence and ease – 3 back flips in a row with the last 2 back flips being no handed, known as a layout. The front aerial skill a free forwards walkover was linked well to a straddle jump, and half turning split jump. Jennifers dismount was a confident round off double tuck back somersault.

The difficulty of her performance was good, her dance was entertaining, but her execution was lacking due to a couple of balancing problems.

Name	Score
Jennifer Gadirova	13.300

Jessica Gadirova on the beam

Like her sister, she got on the beam with a backwards aerial flip. After mounting the beam, she executed a front aerial forwards walk over connected to a straddle jump. She performed her acrobatic series which was a back flip into 2 consecutive layouts. The dismount was a round off double piked back somersault which she landed with a little step. Her difficulty was good, but like her sister, she had balancing problems that would affect her execution points.

Name	Score
Jessica Gadirova	12.866

Amelie Morgan on the beam

Amelie executed a round off layout to mount the beam. She then executed the back flip, layout, layout acrobatic series with confidence and ease. Her dance series was a change leg spit leap, into a change leg split leap with half turn, straight into a Korbut flip (a backward flip to land with the beam in between her legs, first performed by Olga Korubut in 1972. Amelie then performed a double wolf spin, which requires a lot of balance and special awareness from the gymnasts. She displayed a couple of hesitation in her connections meaning she wouldn't have gotten the bonus points. She discounted the beam with a double twist and a solid landing

Name	Score
Amelie Morgan	13.033

Alice Kinsella on the Beam

Beam and bars were considered Kinsella's stronger pieces however her performance on the day of qualification was not her best. She executed a difficult acrobatic series, an aerial side flip, into 2 consecutive layouts, unfortunately there was an alignment issue and she fell off the beam. After composing herself she mounted the beam again and continued with her routine but it was clear she had lost her confidence and the execution of her remaining skills were wobbly, which was costly in deductions. Alice also fell on her dismount on bars.

Jennifer Gadirova on the floor

The Gadirova twins, especially Jennnifer, are known for their entertaining performances on the floor. She chose "rock this joint" as her music, and she started with a short dance before breaking into a run to execute a double layout with a full twist, she completed with astep on landing. After an expressive dance performance and multiple jump and leap series with excellent height. She finished the routine with a single front walk out layout into a round off and a double tuck. It was an excellent performance.

Name	Score
Jennifer Gadirova	13.800

Amelie Morgan on the floor

Amelie Morgan on the floor was excellent in dance. She performed a double layout plus a single tuck to begin her routine. She danced and performed a single turn on one leg. Her execution was good, but she didn't aim for much in terms of difficulty points, which affected her score.

Name	Score
Amelie Morgan	12.466

Jessica Gadirova on the floor

Jessica started her performance seated on the ground before performing a beautiful dance section that was quite elegant to watch. Jessica is a strong tumbler and showed some difficult skills with fantastic execution and almost perfect landings. Her double twisting, double layout had brilliant height and she stuck the tumble with ease. Her final tumble series was a full twisting front somersault into a round off, back flip and double somersault.

Name	Score
Jessica Gadirova	14.033

Amelie Morgan on the uneven bars

After an easy hop to catch the higher bar, Amelie lifted herself up to execute a single reverse grip forward giant swing on the bar, straight into a piked jaeger somersault. She changed bars a total of four times, losing form only when performing a full twisting pak salto transitioning to the lowerbar . She landed the dismount with ease and overall it was a strong routine.

Name	Score
Amelie Morgan	13.833

Rhythmic Group All-round Qualification

The qualification rounds for the Tokyo games took place on day 15 of the games. Team GB was not part of the competition as they had failed to reach this stage. Nevertheless, this performance was so impressive that it warrants a mention.

14 teams competed; 10 would go through, while 4 would drop out at the end of the qualification rounds. The 14 teams were Italy, Israel, the USA, Brazil, Russia Olympic Committee (ROC), Uzbekistan, China, Japan, Ukraine, Belarus, Azerbaijan, Egypt, Australia, and Bulgaria.

The games took place at the Ariake gymnastics centre, and everyone was well aware that the last five gold medals for rhythmic gymnastics had gone to the ROC, making them the team to beat.

The judges arrived at the mostly empty stadium and took the seats at their designated locations from where they could see the upcoming performances. China was the first country to perform at the competition. Five young gymnasts walked onto the floor. They wore emerald and gold while holding white balls that would be a part of their performance. Their coaches walked up behind them, clearly anxious about how their protégés would perform. The coaches held each other's hands, perhaps to comfort each other. The team was composed of Guo Qiqi, Hao Ting, Liu Xin, Xu Yanshi, and Huang Zhangjiagang.

The team had chosen to use traditional Chinese music mixed with modern elements as part of their performance, and it melded perfectly with their routine. The Chinese are known for their high degree of precision dance routines elegantly combined with smoothly choreographed and complimentary movements.

As the white balls went up into the air in perfect unison, the Chinese team would use the limited time to perform tough and complicated manoeuvres before the ball would inevitably come down to the ground to a willing recipient. As their performance progressed, it was obvious to everyone watching that this was an amazing start to the day with an amazing and captivating display.

The next team on the floor was the Australian team wearing pink and gold and holding orange balls. The team was composed of Emily Abbot, 24, Alexandra Aristoteli, 24, Alana Mathews, 22, Himeka Onada, 23, and Felicity White, 20. A fun fact about the Australian team is that they named their dance routines after various animals indigenous to Australia, like the Koala and the wombat, a small sign of their patriotic feelings.

Their performance started pretty well with some nice pop accompanying music but quickly took a wrong turn after one of the team members lost a ball after it slipped from her hands. She froze for a moment but then regained her composure. The team members then had to determine when the most opportune time to get a replacement ball would be, or else they might ruin the entire routine. Someone quickly picked up a white ball placed at the edge of the floor. The replacement ball was a different color from the other balls, a constant reminder of the mistake made. The rest of their performance was not entirely inspiring, but this can be forgiven, given that getting to this level of the Olympics was considered an accomplishment in and of itself.

The next team on the floor was the Brazilians wearing all white and holding blue balls. The team was made up of Maria Arakaki, 17, Deborah Medrado, 19, Nicole Pircio, 19, Geovanna Santos, 19, and Beatriz Silva, 18. The team chose classical music to accompany their elegant routines involving perfectly coordinated ball exchanges and shoulder rolls. A special aspect of their routines was how the music's bursts, slows, highs, and lows matched their movements, which were difficult to achieve.

As the performance continued, the Brazilians increased their tempo to match the shift of music to a faster electronic music feel. Their stunning performance was almost ruined at the end when a team member lost a ball just before their performance ended, which created a dilemma as to whether points would be deducted or not for the loss.

The next team on display was Uzbekistan wearing white, red, and blue and holding red balls. The team was represented by Kseniia Aleksandrova, 20, Kamola Irnazarova, 19, Dinara

Ravshanbekova, 21, Sevara Safoeva, 18, and Nilfar Shomarodova, 22.

As in the case of the Chinese, the Uzbekistani team also chose to start their performance with traditional, slow Uzbekistani music before moving into gentle piano and some moonlight Densetsu towards the end. The team displayed impressive ball exchanges at vast distances and using body difficulties like capturing balls with their feet and punching balls with their backs.

The next team on the floor was the Italians dressed in white, red, and black, holding red balls. Team members included Agnes Duranti, 20, Alessia Maurelli, 24, Daniela Mogurean, 20, Martina Santandrea, 21, and Martina Centofanti, 23. The team chose fast-paced music to match their rapid movements, including straight jumps to catch airborne balls, scissor leaps, and cartwheels.

Qualifier scores for women's rhythmic gymnastics

Rank	Name	Score
1	Bulgaria	91.80
2	ROC	89.05
3	Italy	87.15
4	Israel	84.65
5	China	83.60
6	Ukraine	82.70
7	Japan	79.72
8	Belarus	79.65

AA/Individual Finals

Women's artistic individual all-round finals

The most esteemed title in Olympic gymnastics is the artistic individual all-around. The finals took place on 26th July 2021. Jutta Verkest of Belgium was the youngest competitor at the age of 15 years and 9 months while Kim Bull of Germany was the oldest at 32 years of age.

Despite finishing first in the qualifying rounds, Simone Biles pulled out of the competition and so Jade Carey took her place. Team GB was represented by the Gadirova twins.

The individual finals score table

Rank	Name	Country	Vault	Uneven bars	Balance beam	Floor	Total
1	Sunisa Lee	USA	14.600	15.300	13.833	13.700	57.433
2	Rebecca Andrade	Brazil	15.300	14.666	13.666	13.666	57.298
3	Angelina Melnikova	ROC	14.633	14.900	13.700	13.966	57.199
10	Jessica Gadirova	GB	14.566	13.666	12.033	13.700	53.965
13	Jennife	GB	13.8	12.40	12.933	13.8	53.5

	r Gadirova		00	0		00	33

Women's Floor Finals

After making it into the finals of the artistic floor gymnastics, the 8 contenders walked into the arena looking confident and happy. The contenders were Jade Carey USA, Vanessa Ferrari Italy, Murakami Mai Japan, Angelina Melnikova Russia, Rebecca Andrade Brazil, Jessica Gadirova GB, Jennifer Gadirova GB, and Viktoriia Listunova Russia.

Jennifer had technically not made it into the finals because she was actually in the 9th position in the qualifications. Jennifer was part of the reserve and was added to the finals list after Simone Biles dropped out.

Everyone in the finals was more than capable of getting a medal. What would determine the top three positions was a simple matter of who wanted it most. Sheer determination was the key, and mistakes were not acceptable at this stage.

Viktoriia Listunova

The first competitor to take her place was Russia's Viktoriia Listunova wearing pink and silver. She started by stretching her hands and neck with a look of equal parts determination and anxiety in her eyes. She stood at the corner of the floor, and with Russian music playing in the background, she raised her hands and crossed her legs.

She then proceeded to run forward to generate enough momentum to perform a double layout. Unfortunately, she had too much momentum and stepped out of the mat with both feet, incurring a costly deduction from the judges. She then performed a full turn on her left foot before latching forward to attempt three turns which failed as she had no choice but to use her hands to keep from falling due to a lack of sufficient rotation. Despite her strong choreography, there was no doubt that the two mistakes performed would affect her awarded points.

D score	E score	Penalty	Total score
5.2	7.300	0.100	12.400

Jade Carrey

Next came Jade Carrey of the USA. She started with a beautiful artistic display before performing a double-twisting and double layout. She then slowed down again to perform beautiful artistic poses before performing a double twist and a double tuck. This brilliant stunt was only slightly off due to a difficult landing.

D score	E score	Penalty	Total score
6.3	8.066		14.366

Jessica Gadirova

The third performance was by Jessica Gadirova, and she wore white, blue, and red. Her music of choice was "stereotypes" by Black Violin. It sounded both fast-paced yet refined and merged well with her performance.

In the end, she was awarded 14.000 points, and when the announcement came over the loudspeakers, she clutched her fists and smiled, knowing that she had done her country proud. Her position was now second, just behind Jade Carey and the question on everyone's mind was whether she would be able to hold on to it by the end of the performances by the other competitors.

D score	E score	Penalty	Total score
5.6	8.400		14.000

Angelina Melnikova

The fourth performance came from Angelina Melnikova of Russia. She is known for being clean and precise in all her performances, even at the expense of boldness and creativity. She performed a full-in double layout and scored 14.16 points.

D score	E score	Penalty	Total score
5.9	8.266		14.166

Vanessa Ferrari

The next gymnast was Vanessa Ferrari of Italy; her performance was highly anticipated. She started her performance with perfectly executed double twisting-double layout, moving to beautiful instrumental music. Despite having a history of multiple ankle surgeries, she performed amazing performances with perfect landings that were absolutely flawless. At 30 years of age, her art artistic display was just as good, and when she was done, it was obvious to her and everyone else that she had nailed it. Her coach hugged her tightly, and she was warmly received at the bench.

D score	E score	Penalty	Total score
5.9	8.300		14.200

Murakami Mai

Next came Murakami Mai of Japan, who started with a triple wolf spin; a spin with a leg up followed by a two a half spin; she displayed both good form and strong landings on her tumble series. At this point of the competition, it felt like there were far too few medals that could be awarded to such an awesome ensemble of talent. She received 14.16 points.

D score	E score	Penalty	Total score
5.9	8.266	0.0	14.166

Rebecca Andrade

Next on the list was Rebecca Andrade of Brazil, who has had three knee surgeries in her past. Wearing white, pink, and gold, she walked onto the stage smiling and determined. She started her routine with a diagonal and straight set of double front tucks and aerial cartwheels, which unfortunately ended with her stepping outside the Mat, meaning a 0.1 penalty deduction. The rest of her artistic performance was well in touch with the music of Johan Sebastian Bach's Fug.

D score	E score	Penalty	Total score
5.9	8.233	0.100	14.003

Jennifer Gadirova

The final performance was by Jennifer Gadirova, who looked sure of herself and ready for the challenge. She started her routine with beautiful artistic movements with her hands and turns of her body before attempting a double layout with full twist which didn't go quite as well as she had hoped because her landing was unstable. She quickly recovered and went on to perform a double layout, and later a double tuck back somersault. Her performance showed great elevation and had many leaps and jumps. However, in the end, it was clear that she had made too many small errors in her performance which would take her out of the title run.

D score	**E score**	**Penalty**	**Total score**
5.1	8.133		13.233

The finals score table

Position	Name	Points
1 Gold	Jade Carey USA	14.366
2 Silver	Vanessa Ferrari Italy	14.200
3 Bronze	Murakami Mai Japan	14.166
3 Bronze	Angelina Melnikova Russia	14.166
5	Rebecca Andrade Brazil	14.033
6	Jessica Gadirova GB	14.000
7	Jennifer Gadirova GB	13.233
8	Viktoriia Listunova Russia	12.400

Interestingly, Mai Murakami and Angelina Melnikova had identical E- and D-scores. This meant the tie was unbroken as per FIG's tie-breaking procedures, hence why they had to share the bronze medal.

Team Final Bronze Medal Moment

The finals for all-round team gymnastics took place at Ariake Gymnastics stadium. The atmosphere was both tense and exciting at the same. The young gymnasts walked into the arena accompanied by their coaches and ready to make their mark on history. The teams were arrayed as follows;

- **ROC** - Viktoria Listunova, Lilia Akhaimova, Vladislava Urazova, Angelina Melnikova,

- **USA** - Grace McCallum, Jordan Chiles, Sunisa Lee, Simone Biles

- **China** - Tang Xijing, Zhang Jin, Lu Yufei, Ou Yushan

- **France** - Marine Boyer, Melanie dos Santos, Aline Friess, Carolann Heduit

- **Belgium** - Jutta Verkest, Lisa Vaelen, Nina Derwael, Maellyse Brassart

- **Great Britain** - Amelie Morgan, Alice Kinsella, Jessica Gadirova, Jennifer Gadirova,

- **Italy** - Martina Maggio, Vanessa Ferrari, Asia D'Amato, Alice D'Amato,

- **Japan** - Aiko Sugihara, Mai Murakami, Yuna Hiraiwa, Hitomi Hatakeda

Under normal circumstances, the team to fear would have been the USA, simply because of Simone Biles. However, this was not the case here because she displayed some uncharacteristic weaknesses in the competition so far. This gave other teams the confidence to aim to get the gold medal instead of settling for silver or bronze.

• *Nina Derwael*

The first performance was on the beam by Nina Derwael of Belgium. After an elegant work up, she made a run towards the beam and made a nice round-off layout as a mount. She chose to keep her routine simple and precise rather than complicated and likely to lead to mistakes. She performed two backwards leaps that showed lovely extension. To build up connection bonuses for the difficulty score, she combined acrobatic and gymnastic attributes into her routine. She also executed several single-leg twists on the beam to get dance difficulty points and elegantly dismounted.

Name	Difficulty	Execution	Penalty	Total
Nina	5.600	8.266	0.00	13.866

- **Angelina Melnikova**

The second one on the list was Angelina Melnikova for the vault competition. She performed a double twisting Yurchenko, which is an easy routine for her as she has executed it many times.

Name	Difficulty	Execution	Penalty	Total
Angelina	5.400	9.200	0.0	14.600

- **Grace MC Cullum**

The third gymnast was Grace for the United States, also on the vault. She made a run for the vault and then made a round-off onto the vault. She did a single twist before her hands gently pushed off the table and performed two more aerial twists before making a slightly inelegant landing.

Name	Difficulty	Execution	Penalty	Total
Grace	5.400	9.000	-0.1	14.300

• Hitomi Hitakeda

Fourth in line was Hitomi of Japan, competing on the floor exercise. After a short dance, she executed a well executed first tumble pass, danced again, and then executed three single-leg twists on her left leg. She also executed multiple scissor leaps before ending her routine. She was clearly trying to earn as many difficulty points as possible, but it was obvious that her execution was somewhat lacking.

Name	Difficulty	Execution	Penalty	Total
Hitomi	5.300	7.500	0.0	12.800

• Lilia Akhaimova

Next was Lilia of Russia, and she executed a 'Cheng' vault. This is a very tough manoeuvre rarely attempted, even by the most experienced gymnasts. She executed the move very well.

Name	Difficulty	Execution	Penalty	Total
Lilia	5.800	8.933	0.0	14.733

• Simone Biles

Next on the list was the living legend Simone Biles on the vault for Team USA. She chose to go for the Amanar, which is a move that falls into the Yurchenko family. The move consists of a round-off onto the springboard, then a back handspring onto a vaulting platform, and into 2½ twists in a back layout salto off the table. Very few gymnasts are able to perform this vault.

Name	Difficulty	Execution	Penalty	Total
Simone	5.8	8.766	0.0	13.766

• Tang Xijing

The first person on uneven bars was Tang Xi Jing of China. She changed bars three times using multiple shoot overs to change from the high bar to the low bar plus double ley outs. She displayed excellent and perfectly executed releases.

Name	Difficulty	Execution	Penalty	Total
Tang	6.000	8.500	0.0	14.500

• Carolann Heduit

Carolann of France was next on the bars. She used a straddle back entry and proceeded with an impressive reverse hop from the low bar to the high bar and, after multiple bar exchanges, finished with a double front.

Name	Difficulty	Execution	Penalty	Total
Carolann	5.800	7.666	0.0	13.466

• Asia Dimato

Next was Asia Dimato of Italy on the floor exercise. She started with a strong double layout to open her floor routine. After a short beautiful dance, she proceeded to execute an Arabian double front. She executed multiple aerial scissor leaps before ending her routine with a beautiful dance.

Name	Difficulty	Execution	Penalty	Total
Asia	5.200	7.966	0.0	13.166

• Jennifer Gadirova

The first person to represent Team GB was Jennifer Gadirova on the beam. After a series of good connectives to mount the beam, she executed three lay outs. She added several aerial splits to her routine before a high double tuck and dismounted from the beam.

Name	Difficulty	Execution	Penalty	Total
Jennifer	5.200	8.100	0.0	13.300

• *Melanie de Jesus*

Melanie of France was next on the uneven bars. She started with elegant catch and release moves on the high bars and displayed excellent swings. She executed several pirouettes, which are sometimes hard for her if past deductions are anything to go by.

Name	**Difficulty**	**Execution**	**Penalty**	**Total**
Melanie	6.100	8.100	0.0	14.200

• *Lu Yufei*

Next was Yufei of China on the uneven bars. She didn't have a good performance here because, after a series of pirouettes, she lost her grip on the bars early in her performance. This led to point deductions. She got back on the bars and continued her routine.

Name	Difficulty	Execution	Penalty	Total
Lu	6.100	7.233	0.0	13.333

This marked the end of the first part of the finals competition.

• *Hiraiwa Yuna*

Next was Yuna of Japan for the vault. She ran towards the vault and executed a Yurchenko with one and a half twist.

Name	Difficulty	Execution	Penalty	Total
Yuna	5.000	8.900	0.0	13.900

The Rest of the British Performances in the Finals

• *Jennifer Gadirova*

Jennifer on the floor is known to be an entertaining performer, and she didn't disappoint. After a full-in double lay out, she had a short dance before executing multiple air splits. She executed a final double layout and a double tuck.

Name	Difficulty	Execution	Penalty	Total
Jennifer	5.400	8.400	-0.1	13.700

(Immediately after Jennifer Gadirova's performance, an announcement came over the PA stating that Simone Biles would not continue with the competition.)

• *Amelie Morgan*

On the uneven bars for Team GB was Amelie Morgan. She executed her bar changes flawlessly, plus strong pirouettes and circles for an excellent performance.

Name	Difficulty	Execution	Penalty	Total
Amelie	-	-	-	14.433

• *Jessica Gadirova*

On the vault for Team GB was Jessica Gadirova. After a powerful run, she executed an excellent Yurchenko with double twist. Her landing was elegant and precise.

Name	Difficulty	Execution	Penalty	Total
Jennifer	5.400	9.033	0.0	14.433

• *Alice Kinsella*

After her disappointment in the qualifying rounds Alice was able to recover quickly from her ankle injury and get back to the competition arena. As the oldest member of the GB team her experience was vital for the rest of the team. Her dance performance was beautiful, but she lacked precision in her consecutive tumble passes.

Name	Difficulty	Execution	Penalty	Total
Alice	-	-	-	12.800

Summary

The day had started a little a rough for GB because Amelie Morgan took a tumble in her first performance but the team were able to regain their composure and so by midway through the competition, GB ranked in 7th place. The vault was the team's best piece of the day as Alice, Jessica and Jennifer all performed double twisting Yurchenko vaults, and each of them scored over 14.000. This moved the team from 7th place to 5th place which obviously meant that they were within grasp of a medal.

To have a shot at clinching a medal the team knew that had to finish strong. After Jessica had already scored a 13.566 on the uneven bars and Alice had scored a 14.166, the last member of the team to perform was Amelie Morgan. This was her chance to redeem herself after a tough start in the day and she did not disappoint. She scored an impressive 14.033 which put quite a bit of distance between them and their next competitor Italy.

Watching the Italian performance from their seats it was clear to see just how tense GB was. Italy needed 13.591 on the beam to beat Britain but they simply couldn't muster up a good enough performance and so GB took the Bronze medal. When the team saw the scores on the board they broke into tears and celebration. As Alice would later express *"When we saw the scores, I was speechless, on the floor crying, I couldn't hold it in."*

The team finals table results

Rank	Team	Vault	Bars	Beam	Floor	Total
1	ROC	43.799	44.699	39.532	39.532	169.528
	Lilia Akhaimova (ROC)	14.733				
	Viktoria Listunova (ROC)		14.900	14.333	14.166	
	Angelina Melnikova (ROC)	14.600	14.933	12.566	13.966	
	Vladislava Urazova (ROC)	14.466	14.866	12.633	13.366	
2	USA	42.732	43.266	41.232	38.866	166.096

	Simone Biles	13.766				
	Jordan Chiles	14.666	14.166	13.433	11.700	
	Sunisa Lee		15.400	14.133	13.666	
	Grace MC Cullum	14.300	13.700	13.666	13.500	
3	**GB**	**43.132**	**41.765**	**38.866**	**40.333**	**164.096**
	Jennifer Gadirova	14.433		13.300	13.700	
	Jessica Gadirova	14.433	13.566		13.833	
	Alice Kinsella	14.266	14.166	13.333	12.800	
	Amelie Morgan		14.033	12.233		

Interviews From The Team

As is the custom for medal winners at the Olympics, Team GB was interviewed by journalists while seated at a long table. The four young ladies were clearly still emotional after the whole experience, but they wore their bronze medals proudly on their chests.

The interview began with the young ladies asked to make their opening statements regarding what they thought about their victory.

The first person to speak was Jessica Gadirova. As one might imagine, the press was obsessed with the fact that there were identical twins on the same team.

Jessica articulated the fact that she was still in a state of unbelief by stating, *"I just can't believe it. We've made history! We enjoyed ourselves. It's a dream we never thought was possible, but it happened. We just really tried to enjoy the moment and to see our names up there as the third was just ... I'm just speechless. I'm so proud of all these girls. We've worked so hard, and we pushed each other, and this is what it turned out to be. I'm just forever grateful."*

Amelie Morgan was seated left of Jessica, and her demeanour seemed mature and very sophisticated. Her voice was calm, commanding, and happy. She gave her opinion on the day's events stating, *"I think for us going out into this final, I was just kind of aiming to bring the team together and enjoy the experience and take it in. We didn't put any pressure on ourselves to go for that medal, and I think that's kind of made it for us. We went out there, enjoyed ourselves, and did the performances we knew we could do. Obviously, there were some ups and downs, but we pulled it together after my first routine, and we just absolutely smashed it; I am so proud of everyone on this team. Every single person played a role in our securing that medal. All those weeks of hard work ... I'm just so proud of everyone."*

What stood out in her words was that the team didn't really put much pressure on themselves to win the medal, which Amelie Morgan believes was probably the critical factor that led to their success.

Pressure to perform can often lead to unnecessary mistakes, which is why positive and negative upsets often happen at the Olympics. Teams and individuals who everyone expected to win the day can end up losing simply because of the amount of pressure placed upon them. Then teams and individuals who are simply happy to be at the finals and with no expectations of victory can sometimes win the medals. The importance of being relaxed and simply enjoying the moment would be highlighted by the next speaker Alice Kinsella.

Alice Kinsella, seated to the left of Amelie, was next. She began by agreeing with her teammate's assessment. *"Yeah, so we actually came out here to go and enjoy it, get the experience and we did do that. Getting the bronze medal was absolutely amazing. These three girls worked so hard for the past couple of weeks, and they honestly deserved this so much, and I couldn't be more proud of them."*

What stood out in Alice Kinsella's statement was the fact that the team was concerned with getting experience at the tournament rather than necessarily getting a medal. That is because the team was extremely young, and they knew that they could always get another chance in the future or perhaps even two chances.

The next bronze medallist to speak was Jennifer Gadirova, whose demeanour was a bit more serious but still quite proud of their accomplishments. She gave her opinion on the victory, stating, *"This is more than a dream come true; we just came into this competition to do our best; we were so thrilled and happy just to make the final level. So coming away with a medal ... it's just like the other girls said. I'm so proud of them. Our journey hasn't been smooth. We've had bumps on the road; it's just been a roller-coaster, and just being here is an achievement in and of itself. I have no words; it's just amazing, like, we are all so happy and* excited, and we're all just speechless. It's my first medal at how many years, it's a massive achievement, and we are just over the moon."

At this point, the audience got a chance to ask the bronze medallists question. The first question asked the girls to state at what point it dawned on them that they could actually win the medal. Amelie Morgan decided to answer the question. She reiterated that the team didn't really come to the finals with the clear-cut expectation of a medal victory. They understood that gymnastics is one of those sports where an upset can happen at any moment.

She also highlighted that every team made mistakes on the floor, and so they knew that they had to stay focused until the final moment. She also stated that it dawned on them that it was possible to win before their last routine, but they couldn't think about this fact too much.

"After our vault, we knew that we had one piece left, and the scores were very tight, so I think in the back of our minds, we knew that we had to do something special to be up there, but at the same time we knew that we had to focus on our performances and we couldn't think too much about the medals."

An interesting part of the interview was when the second question was raised regarding the selection process used to choose which girls would get to represent their country.

Amelie Morgan's response stood out due to her candour in mentioning the fact that there was criticism towards some of the selection choices for the team. She highlighted that they chose to ignore this as unnecessary noise to focus on giving their best performance. In responding, she said, *"Obviously, there has been a fair bit of criticism on social media, and although we try and put that past us, we know that it's always in the back of our minds. It does stick with you, and I think this kind of gave us that drive to kind of show people what we can do, that we deserve this place, and we came here for a reason. So it does make it worth it when we prove ourselves and the hard work we put in."*

This response highlights an aspect of Olympic competition that has to do with how athletes are treated on social media. We live in an age where everyone has an opinion on everything, and people are not shy about criticizing everything that people do wrong.

For athletes who are still in their teens, being able to handle criticism, vulgarity, and insults thrown your way can be a very tough challenge indeed. Sadly, this is not an issue being discussed enough by professional athletes or the officials responsible for their mental health. The final chapter shall cover a little more of this.

It was clear to see from her answer that Amelie Morgan was a confident sought of girl who would never allow anyone's negative opinion of her to dissuade her from her dreams. More to the point, she highlighted that the criticism actually helped motivate her.

The final question in the interview was directed at all the girls, and it asked how they thought this Bronze medal victory would impact other girls back in Great Britain who watched their performance.

Jessica was first to respond, stating, *"Obviously, we've made history. To be the first GB team to win a medal in gymnastics finals really just shows that it is possible and we've done it. We've inspired so many little girls…"*

Amelie Morgan was next, stating; *"I think coming out here was a dream of ours for so long and to come away with a medal we never would even have dreamed of, and I think it proves that even what seems impossible isn't impossible and you should always reach for those goals no matter how far away they seem."* Amelie Morgan expressed her hope that their impossible dream becoming a reality would inspire young girls all over Britain to believe that they too can accomplish something similar.

Since the victory, the girls have gone on interviews with a couple of internet personalities and news outlets, including Good Morning Britain.

The next and final chapter of this book aims to help offer some tips for practicing gymnasts and some motivation to aspiring gymnastics as to why this sport is a truly remarkable experience.

Chapter 6: Motivation For Aspiring Gymnasts

"Don't ever be afraid to dream too big. Nothing is impossible. If you believe in yourself, you can achieve it."

Nastia Liukin

The previous chapters helped you understand the history of gymnastics as a sport, how the sport developed in Britain, and the successes of the British team at the Olympics.

This final chapter aims to help you understand why getting into this sport could be the best decision of your life, regardless of whether you intend to pursue the sport professionally or not. You will also learn about some challenges you are likely to encounter in the sport and how to overcome them safely.

Why Get Into Gymnastics?

There are several reasons to get into gymnastics. We will look at some of these reasons one at a time.

Improving your physical health

We live in an age where millions of people struggle with lifestyle diseases such as diabetes and high blood pressure.

Finding effective ways of dealing with these problems comes down to whether society can offer effective but enjoyable ways of getting physically healthy.

Here are some ways how gymnastics can help improve your health.

• **Effective weight loss**

The routines found in various artistic gymnastic categories are all capable of helping you burn calories and get in better physical shape. Weight loss is critical in helping reduce the probability of diseases like diabetes or high blood pressure.

Suppose you aren't interested in physically challenging aspects of gymnastics like uneven bars or the pommel horse. In that case, there are always easier versions of gymnastics like floor exercises or rhythmic gymnastics that incorporate a lot of dance into their routines.

• **Building muscle strength**

If one looks at some of the best female gymnasts out there, such as Simone Biles or Jennifer Gadirova, it is obvious that their bodies have a lot more muscles than most women –and even men, for that matter. The sport of gymnastics has several routines that can help you develop strong muscles in the arms, shoulders, and legs. This can be useful in self-defence and being overall healthy.

• Improving bone health

It's not a well-known fact, but bones behave a lot like muscles in the sense that using them makes them stronger while ignoring them makes them weaker.

The manoeuvres involved in gymnastics help prevent bones from becoming weak and brittle. Bones, after all, are living tissue, and when force is exerted upon them, they respond to this by becoming denser and more capable.

• Improving flexibility

Something you can say about gymnasts with absolute certainty is that they are very flexible. Moves like splits, scissor leaps, and aerial cartwheels all work to improve the health and well-being of athletes.

Improving personal discipline

Becoming a good gymnast requires you to be committed to a good schedule. It's impossible to engage in sporadic training routines and expect positive outcomes from this. When a teenage girl gets used to practicing for two or three hours a day every day, they develop a sense of responsibility, commitment, and tenacity that nobody else in their peer group could have. This discipline isn't just crucial for gymnastics but can translate into other aspects of life like academics and careers.

Personal discipline is about getting yourself to perform difficult tasks even if they don't feel good at the moment. It requires perseverance and the ability to delay gratification to achieve great goals in the future.

Executing difficult gymnastics skills also requires emotional control. This is about the ability to stay focused, calm, and single-minded. It is a well-established fact the ability to control one's emotions is the single most critical factor in determining personal and career success.

Improving concentration and accelerating learning

Executing gymnastics routines requires you to focus your mind on the task at hand and think about ways of executing it successfully. When a young, developing teenager engages in gymnastic exercises, it helps develop a stronger mind capable of handling difficult mental challenges. Adults can better focus on their responsibilities, and teens can do better at their academics.

Improves your ability to work with others

Team gymnastic sports help individuals to learn how to communicate with other people. The ability to express one's expectations, concerns, and opinions is a critical life skill that takes practice to develop. Gymnastics as a team sport can play a crucial role in helping you improve your ability to talk to others and coordinate your activities with a productive and seamless manner.

Teaches you the value of patience and growth

It takes time and effort to become good at gymnastics. This is the same for any other useful goal in life. When you train your mind to be patient in pursuing a challenging goal, you are better able to be patient and committed when pursuing future life goals, no matter how tough things get along the way –and they can get pretty tough.

How Gymnastics Empowers Women

As you have seen in previous chapters, the role of women in gymnastics went from being non-existent to a major force to reckon with. This process and development was difficult and required women to be willing to demand equal treatment in the sport. This eventually developed into women participating in major tournaments like the Olympics. Today, a sport that began as a way to train the military is actually far more associated with women than men.

Gymnastics builds up women's confidence

Building an "I can" mentality is one of the most crucial and powerful tools that you can have in your life tool kit. This mind-set can help you take on the challenges that life will throw your way. Gymnastics can help a great deal in this regard.

Each time you learn how to perform a gymnastics move you couldn't do before, you will notice an increase in your sense of self. When you can execute difficult and elegant moves that can awe and entertain crowds of people, it can alter your self-belief and perception of what you can or cannot accomplish.

Gymnastics changes how women are perceived

The common misconception about women is that they are incapable of being physically strong or emotionally resilient enough to take on tough challenges. One of the reasons women weren't allowed in gymnastics in the late 19th century was this wrong perception that women just couldn't handle it.

Today, looking at some of the fittest and strongest gymnasts in the world, nobody can claim that women are not as strong or as capable as men when it comes to physical abilities.

This change in perception regarding women has helped improve women's social standing in society and opened new doors for growth and opportunity. Not too long ago, it was unthinkable that women could serve in the military, but today 11% of the UK's regular forces are women. This is only possible because sports like gymnastics showed that women were just as capable as men when it came to taking on tough challenges.

Gymnastics teaches girls that failure is not permanent

Before you can master even the most basic moves in gymnastics, you will need to fail a great number of times. For many people, failure will often be traumatizing and incapacitating. However, this is not the case for somebody who has engaged in gymnastics.

Each time a gymnast fails at a skill, they learn to pick themselves up, dust off the failure, and try again. This culture of rising up and not letting failure be the end is a valuable life skill to have.

What Would It Take To Get To The Olympics?

Many girls wonder whether they can really get to the Olympics and what it would take. The answer to this question is a definite yes, provided you are determined enough.

The Olympics brings together the best gymnasts in the entire world. These people have dedicated their entire lives and purpose in life to competing on the Olympic Stage. If you want to be at this stage, you have to be as committed as they are.

- *Have a timetable or schedule of some kind*

A schedule is your first and most critical step toward getting to the Olympics. Listening to the success stories of most gymnasts who get to the Olympics, they all commit a minimum of 30 training hours a week, with some taking it as far as 40 hours a week. They do this despite dealing with academic challenges in high school or college.

The only way to accomplish this is to set a schedule and then stick to it as a matter of life and death. Do not ignore training sessions or make excuses for lack of commitment during your sessions.

• *Stay healthy by avoiding unnecessary risks*

Learn to watch out for unnecessary risks to your health. Do not expose yourself to illnesses that can interfere with your training schedule or weaken your body.

• *Be likable*

While choices for who goes to the Olympics come down mostly to merit, there is a certain element that simply comes down to the human element. We tend to favour people who have likable personalities. People who smile and are warm and approachable will naturally have an advantage over cold, unemotional, or rude individuals.

Is There an ideal Gymnast Body?

Many women or girls hoping to get into gymnastics often wonder if they have the right body for the sport. We all know height is an advantage in basketball and arm length is useful in boxing, but what about gymnastics. Are there characteristics that could be advantageous or disadvantageous when engaging in gymnastics? And if these factors exist, can they hinder you from participating in the sport?

The truth is that most gymnasts tend to look short, small, and very muscular. Being tall in gymnastics can be a disadvantage because the strength needed to lift the body and move is greater. Muscles are also needed to perform difficult skills.

The fact that there is an ideal body doesn't mean gymnastics is closed to you if you don't meet the exact specifications. Many very successful gymnasts have been very successful despite being lean or tall. What is really important in gymnastics is understanding your own body and learning how to take advantage of your strengths. Then you need to practice every day until you can perfect your moves.

Find The Right Coach You Trust And Can Work well With

Getting the right coach is one of the most important choices you could make in gymnastics.

A coach will help train you to learn the basics of gymnastics and then how to execute tough gymnastics routines. They will watch your performances to understand your weaknesses so that they can help maximize those strengths and minimize the impact of the weaknesses.

A good coach is a teacher, friend, and mentor. They will push you to be the best and call you out for being late to practice, but they will not be insulting or condescending.

A good coach provides you with emotional support and offers guidance in difficult times. A good coach also places your personal safety above anything else. They will not let you perform moves you are not ready for that might lead to an accident.

A coach should understand what level you are at and only enter you into competitions you can handle. This is important because it can help you grow both in skills and confidence at the right pace. Taking on more than you can handle can be a source of low self-esteem, and it can lead you to quit the sport before you have given it a real chance.

A good coach understands the value of effective communication. That means they must be able to offer you their thoughts and ideas in a way you can understand and relate to.

Finally, it's important to remember that a coach has a lot of power over you, and they can easily misuse that power for their benefit. Do not be afraid to speak out if a coach is abusing the power they have over you.

How to win over your gymnastics coach

Once you have a good coach, you are responsible for ensuring that you can keep them motivated and invested in you.

• Always be on time for training

If there is one thing all coaches hate, its athletes who don't show up for training sessions on time. Once you have a training schedule, make sure you keep to it and do not miss sessions or show up late. If you can't be at training sessions, remember to communicate this information to your coach so that they can prepare to use that time in some other way.

• Take all training sessions seriously

When you arrive for a training session, make sure you are properly dressed as a gymnast and have all the necessary safety gear you will need.

• Listen to their advice

When your coach offers you their opinion, remember that it is based on many years of experience. Don't assume that you know more than them or are smarter. This is especially true as regards matters of safety. When your coach says you are not yet ready to attempt a particular skill, trust the coach's judgment and keep practicing.

• Have a positive attitude

A positive attitude has to do with how you talk, move, and behave when on the job. When you show contempt for the sport and engage in idle chitchat during practice, it shows you are not fully committed to the sport. Remember that your coach will only ever put in as much effort as you. So remember to smile, be polite, don't get upset, and always be ready to admit your mistakes.

How To Avoid Physical Injuries In Gymnastics

In the first chapter, we looked at some of the injuries gymnasts are at risk of incurring. These include shoulder dislocation, wrist injuries, Achilles tendon injury, Anterior Cruciate Ligament (ACL) Injury, and knee cap dislocations.

These risks can threaten your gymnastics career and can result in a lot of pain. Thus, you need to learn ways of preventing injuries when you are practicing to become the best you can be.

• *Always wear safety gear when training*

Gymnastics has a lot of safety gear you can take advantage of, especially when training. This is especially the case when you are trying to learn a new move and are more at risk of injuring yourself.

This safety gear includes hand safety grips to help ensure you don't lose your grip when practicing on the bar, elbow braces to prevent damage to your elbows when you fall, and footwear with a strong enough grip to prevent unnecessary falls when running towards a vault or while on a beam.

• *Have a spotter when learning new moves*

A spotter is someone who stands close to you when you are on a beam, trampoline, or the bars. Their job is to monitor your moves, and if you make a mistake, they will catch you before you hit the ground. Spotters have helped prevent serious injuries to gymnasts. They have to be fast and strong enough to catch you in the second when you have lost control and are at risk.

• *Perform warm-up exercises before a routine*

Warm-up exercises can be a helpful way of preventing injuries because they get your heart beating faster and blood flowing to your muscles quicker. The oxygenation of your muscles primes them for the difficult tasks ahead but without tiring them up.

Warm-ups also raise your body temperature and prevent muscle soreness that emerges from engaging your muscles in strenuous activity without preparing them first. Maintaining Good Mental health While Practicing Gymnastics

- **Inspect equipment before training**

When you are at the training gym, you may not always have full control of the equipment. As such, you need to make sure the equipment you will use is actually in good condition at all times. Otherwise, a loose bar will cause a fall, and an unstable beam could break an ankle.

- **Take time to heal from minor injuries**

In earlier chapters, we highlighted that many gymnasts at the Olympics were able to win medals despite having fractures. While such incidences make good stories to tell, the truth is that it is actually a really bad idea to try and "play through the pain." When you apply pressure and effort onto a broken bone or if you keep using a damaged tendon, you are actually making the situation much worse than it already is. The more pressure you apply, the worse the damage gets, and you could easily end up being unable to play in the future. Your best option is to see a doctor and allow your body to rest and heal.

- **Always have a first aid kit close by**

A first aid kit can help with injury by reducing pain and stopping bleeding. The medical assistance you receive immediately after an injury can help prevent the more serious damage likely to occur if you have to wait to get to a doctor.

- ***Remember to stay hydrated***

Drinking water three hours before your workout will help focus your mind better. Water also helps prevent injuries to your muscles and keeps you from making unnecessary mistakes due to a lack of focus.

- ***Pay attention to your body and trust your instincts***

If you feel like something is off with your body, pay attention to that gut feeling. Take a day off or see a doctor or physiotherapist for a routine check-up. The earlier a problem is detected, the better your chances of getting the problem fixed.

Gymnastics And Good Mental Health

Even the best athletes, such as Gymnast Simone Bileshave suffered from mental health issues due to the stress associated with their respective sports. That is why it is critical to monitor your psychological health and make sure you have someone who loves you more than they love the success in your gymnastics career watching over your mental health.

When Simone Biles pulled out of her routines in the Tokyo Olympics, the world was shocked because she looked so strong, and nobody thought gymnastics could take such a toll on someone's psychological health. The truth is that a failure to monitor your emotions and thoughts can easily lead to a breakdown.

Here are some tips for staying psychological healthy as you pursue a life in gymnastics:

• *Don't put too much pressure on yourself*

Putting excessive pressure on yourself is the single biggest risk factor that could cause psychological health problems. You need to have a positive and happy career in gymnastics, which can only come if you aren't constantly berating yourself for every mistake you make. That doesn't mean you should be apathetic or have low ambition. It just means you should understand that not everything will be perfect at all times and that you won't win every competition or have a good day every day. Moderating your expectations can make you better able to handle the sport's many challenges.

- ***Don't read social media comments about yourself***

Social media has been one of mankind's greatest and worst inventions. A comment that stood out during Amelie Morgan's interview after winning the bronze medal was that they had been hurt by comments made on social media regarding whether they were worthy to represent their country at the Olympics.

Criticism is the one thing never lacking on social media. Reading comments of people who have no idea what it takes to perform gymnastics routines can lead you to be depressed or angry.

It's not just social media, but the internet –as a whole– can negatively impact your self-esteem. If you are lucky enough to participate in gymnastic local or national tournaments, there is a good chance there will be articles written about your performance. Some of these articles will be negative, so it is probably a good idea to ignore them all.

- ***Set goals you know you can achieve***

You must understand that while it is important to set goals to help keep you motivated, you must always keep the goals within the realm of possibility. You have to factor in your age, body type, and time constraints to determine what goals are feasible and which ones are not. Then remember to be patient in your pursuit of these goals. Remember that Rome was not built in a day, and you won't achieve world-class gymnastic performances in a day either. Take things one step at a time, and you will eventually reach the highest levels possible.

- ***Talk to someone about your fears and concerns***

One of the best moves you can make in any sporting career is always having someone around you who you can talk to when you feel afraid, disappointed, or unmotivated. This will help you to overcome negative feelings which would otherwise overwhelm you.

When you fail to talk about issues bothering you, they can compound over time and take their toll not just on your personal life but your professional one as well.

The best person to talk to is someone who cares more about you as a person rather than you as an athlete. A parent, older sibling, or professional therapists are all good options to consider.

- ***Surround yourself with supportive people and avoid negative ones***

Stay away from people who are always telling you negative things. People who constantly criticize, make jokes, or tell you that you are wasting your time are all dangerous to have around you. They can destroy your self-esteem and keep you from overcoming tough challenges when you meet them.

You want to surround yourself with people who love you and want the best for you. People who communicate their confidence in you even when you have lost faith in yourself are the best to have around you. These people will be your light to see you through the dark times inevitably ahead.

- ***Have a life outside of gymnastics that gives you joy***

When all you think about at all times is gymnastics, you will fatigue your brain, which will lead to a decline in interest and motivation. That is why it is important to have activities not related to gymnastics that allow you to relax and enjoy life. Hobbies like swimming, singing, baking, and walking your dog can all help to keep your mind fresh and at peace. When you eventually return to gymnastics, you will find that things are much easier, and you will execute your routines with greater fluency and accuracy.

- ***Balance your personal responsibilities with your gymnastics life***

If you have personal responsibilities at home or school, they should never lag because of your gymnastics life. When there is a lack of proper balance between your gymnastics life and the rest of your personal life, it can be a potential point of stress and conflict. That means you should take enough time to ensure your relationships with the people who love you, such as your parents and siblings, are healthy.

Tips For Becoming The Best

Becoming the best in gymnastics is what you will need to do if you ever hope to participate in international competitions such as the Olympics. This will not be easy and will require a lot of effort.

There are a few tips you can make a part of your life that can greatly improve your odds of getting the best out of yourself.

1. Eat healthily

You are what you eat is an old cliché, but that doesn't make the expression any less true. When you are on a gymnastics floor, you will need strong muscles, strong bones, and a sharp mind.

Perhaps the biggest factor determining the condition of your boy will be what you eat. That means you need to speak to a nutritionist or an informed coach on what the best kind of diet for you is going to be.

• For strong bones

A good diet for strong bones should include Calcium, Vitamin D, and magnesium. These nutrients are crucial for bone healing after injury and bone strength to avoid those injuries in the first place. A gymnast with brittle bones won't last long in the game.

Here are a couple of foods rich in calcium; cheese, kale soya, bread, yogurt, beans, and trout.

Here are foods rich in Magnesium; nuts, seeds, dry beans, whole grains, wheat, and oat bran.

The best source of Vitamin D is the sun. You should get some sun in the morning and late afternoon. Do not expose yourself to the sun at mid-day because you won't get much Vitamin D from it, and you are likely just damaging your skin. In the UK it is recommended for children and adults to take a Vitamin D supplement in the autumn and winter months due to lack of sun exposure.

• For strong muscles

Muscle tissue is what you will need for strong hands and strong feet. To get strong muscles, you need to eat foods rich in protein. The best sources of protein are as follows; eggs, dairy, fish, beans, tuna, pasta, lentils, nuts, seeds, black beans, and broccoli.

• For a sharp mind

Complex gymnastic skills require you to think extremely fast and adapt to your own mistakes while mid-air or on a beam. To do this, your brain's processing power should be functioning at maximum efficiency. Therefore, you should make sure your diet guarantees that the neurons in your brain are healthy.

The best foods to boost concentration are fatty fish, eggs, coffee, nuts, leafy vegetables, pumpkin seeds, and green tea. Try berries, turmeric, dark chocolate, avocado, and olive to boost your intelligence.

2. Build a support system, and don't be afraid to ask for help

When you feel overwhelmed or struggle to learn a particular skill, do not be afraid to admit your weaknesses and ask for help from the people around you. By failing to ask for help, you put your physical and psychological health at risk.

The only way to overcome this problem is to build an effective support system around you. Make friends with other gymnasts who understand what you are going through and can help you navigate the challenges you are facing. Get emotional support from your family and make time for them even as you pursue your gymnastic dreams.

3. Be consistent

The ability to be consistent is the key to success at a high level of gymnastics. This means your focus and attention need to be on your craft: it should be the single most important aspect of your life. This means you can't miss practice just because you feel like it.

4. Set short term goals before long term goals

A common mistake many gymnasts make is that they set goals for what they hope to achieve in a year or even a decade. A better approach is to set small goals and then use the successes of these goals to work towards achieving greater objectives.

Train yourself to achieve goals over the course of a day, three days, a week, and at most, a fortnight. Shorter time scales force you to focus on whether you are making progress towards improving your skills or not.

A day to a week is enough to teach you a basic to intermediate skill. Each skill you learn is a stepping stone to greatness. When you work towards achieving seemingly small goals, these small victories accumulate, and you eventually achieve far greater goals, such as getting to the Olympics.

5. Learn how to deal with the yips aka twisties or mental block

The yips are neither a myth nor are they a joke. They have ended the professional careers of some of the best athletes in a wide array of sports such as golf, boxing, basketball, and gymnastics.

The term yips is popularly attributed to Tommy Armour, a professional golfer before he used the term to explain why he stopped playing the sport professionally.

We can define the yips as a sudden and inexplicable inability to execute previously easy tasks. This loss of fine motor control causes athletes to lose their ability to perform tasks as well as they could before.

In gymnastics, the yips are usually referred to as the twisties or a mental block. They manifest as an inability to maintain body control when performing aerial manoeuvres. Many gymnasts who have suffered from this condition have described it as an almost out-of-body experience. Things that were easy suddenly become difficult or impossible. Gymnasts have reported feeling disoriented or even losing awareness of where the ground is. Coaches will advise taking a bit of time off when a gymnast has the yips because they can result in serious bodily injury.

It has been said that Simone Biles experienced the yips in the Tokyo games, which is what led her to drop out. American gymnasts Laurie Hernandez and Aleah Finnegan have described having suffered from the twisties at different points in their careers.

So what causes the yips?

It's not entirely known what causes the yips. One theory is that muscle spasms occur due to the overuse of certain muscles leading to some form of fatigue. This theory isn't perfect either because even after athletes have taken a long break, they still aren't able to overcome the yips.

Another theory is that they are simply the result of an aging body. However, this theory doesn't entirely fit because even very young gymnasts like Bryony Page have reported experiencing the yips.

Perhaps the most compelling theory that explains the yips is that they result from fear building up in the subconscious mind. Sometimes we are afraid and can't admit the fear to ourselves and others. Fear is seen as weakness, and so we often push fear out of our conscious mind, but this doesn't stop it from festering and growing in the subconscious mind. This fear leads to a conflict within your mind and results in your body fighting you instead of being able to control it.

The most common source of fear for competitive athletes is that people will see them fail. This is especially the case for athletes at the highest level of any sport. When you have already reached the top, there is only one place left to go: down. This fear of failing and being mocked or criticized for not being the best can lead to a build up of fear that results in a self-fulfilling prophecy. Your fear of failure thus leads to your failure.

Signs you have the yips include;

- An inability to focus

- A lack of awareness when performing aerial moves

- Inability to grasp the bar properly

- Persistent slip-ups

- Inexplicable spasms in your hands or legs

- Difficulty executing previously basic skills

<u>Dealing with yips</u>

Perhaps there is some truth that muscle fatigue might play a role in developing the yips. Therefore, the first objective is to make sure you get some rest.

As you rest, take time to introspect and consider the possibility that there is something in your professional or personal life that is making you afraid.

Perhaps it could be the fear of failing in front of other people. It might be a personal fear, such as conflicts with loved ones or falling grades at school.

Whatever the problem plaguing you might be, you are the only person capable of finding it and working through it. Dream analysis can also be very helpful in finding what your subconscious mind is truly afraid of.

Conclusion

Gymnastics isn't just a sport; it is a life experience. The lessons you will learn in this sport will change you forever. You will also develop an inner strength that you never knew you had. This strength will allow you to overcome challenges all through your life that you would not have been able to otherwise. The sport will help you meet amazing people who are just as determined and committed as you are. Remember to cherish these relationships, whether they are with your coaches or your fellow athletes.

This sport is supposed to be enjoyable above all else. A common theme among the best gymnasts is that they love the sport in and of itself rather than for the medals or glory. Remember to enjoy what you are doing and observe the safety tips you've learned, so you are always fit and healthy.

I wish you the best of luck in your future gymnastics journey, whether you are a gymnast, coach, judge or parent.

Printed in Great Britain
by Amazon